MEMOS TO THE GOVERNOR

T0352133

MEMOS TO THE GOVERNOR

An Introduction to State Budgeting

Third Edition

Dall W. Forsythe

and

Donald J. Boyd

GEORGETOWN UNIVERSITY PRESS
Washington, DC

© 2012 Georgetown University Press. All rights reserved.
No part of this book may be reproduced or utilized in any form
or by any means, electronic or mechanical, including
photocopying and recording, or by any information storage and
retrieval system, without permission in writing from the publisher.

Library of Congress Cataloging-in-Publication Data

Forsythe, Dall W., 1943-
Memos to the governor : an introduction to state budgeting /
Dall W. Forsythe and Donald J. Boyd. — 3rd ed.
p.   cm.
Includes bibliographical references and index.
ISBN 978-1-58901-924-9 (pbk. : alk. paper)
1. Budget—United States—States. 2. Finance, Public—
United States—States. I. Boyd, Donald J. II. Title.
HJ2053.A1F67 2012
352.4'82130973—dc23
2011052062

This book is printed on acid-free paper meeting the
requirements of the American National Standard for
Permanence in Paper for Printed Library Materials.
15 14 13 12   9 8 7 6 5 4 3 2
First printing

Contents

Foreword to the Second Edition

I have been a student for most of my adult life. I taught in law school for more than a decade, lectured on government and politics for much longer than that, and was governor of New York for twelve years. In all that time, I have not read a more insightful, useful, and valuable description of what is perhaps the single most important function in government—the making of a budget—than *Memos to the Governor*. Thanks to its format, which is a series of brief memoranda, and the clear and cogent language in which it is written, the sometimes arcane political and technical realities at work in the budget process are rendered comprehensible, if not entirely palatable. Anyone interested in how governments work should read and study this updated edition.

Let me add that I am not promising that it will make the task of budget making easy: No book will do that. Accomplished accounting professionals are essential to a good budget-making process, but making a budget for the federal government, the state of New York, or any other governmental entity requires many other skills and experience as well. Meeting the requirement to create a balanced budget for the state of New York is probably the principal objective of the budget director, not of the governor or the legislature. Those elected officials have been constitutionally assigned the task of raising and dispensing resources to meet the needs of the population, which cannot reasonably be met by their own private efforts. Abraham Lincoln described the role with characteristic cogency: "Government is the coming together of people to do for one another collectively what they could not do as well as or at all privately."

Our government encourages the free enterprise system, but even Adam Smith was forced to admit that a well-run market system is not enough to ensure a reasonably sound society. That higher objective requires interventions in the market system that redistribute people's wealth to provide facilities and benefits not otherwise available. Public schools are a good example, as are hospitals, affordable housing, prisons, highways, mass transit, space travel, armies, militias, and a host of competing program needs.

So the starting point in making a good budget is reaching intelligent conclusions as to what people need and want from government and how to pay for them. If you are a governor, the difficulty in paying for them will depend on the economy at both the federal and state levels. It is difficult for the state government alone to produce an economy that is strong enough to supply the wealth that, reasonably taxed, would give all that the people of the state need and want. As the book points out, although a budget can influence the state economy positively or negatively, it is fair to say that the success of a governor principally depends upon the condition of the federal economy during his or her term of office.

During the second half of the 1990s, governors in large states such as New York were like surfboard riders being carried blithely along the top of a giant wave of abundance created by the federal economy. The wave flooded state treasuries with money and political power: Governors could cut taxes and spend lavishly at the same time—a miracle marriage for political executives. But once the wave subsided in the beginning of the new millennium, governors found themselves fishing in shallow waters.

In 2002, very soon after booking the largest surplus in its history, the federal government fell precipitously into deficit, dragging virtually every state and local government behind it. In calendar year 2003 they were faced cumulatively with a $100 billion debt. The entire period that Dall Forsythe and I spent together in Albany some years earlier was also a difficult time that began and ended with a recession, with only a few years of strong revenue flow to pay for all the good things with which we wanted to supply our state without having to raise taxes. If making a budget had been simply a matter of ensuring that what goes out in expenditures does not exceed what comes in as revenues, it would not have made much difference how weak the economy was. All we would have needed to do was to spend less or raise taxes, and I could have done that without Dall. The problem was that a neatly symmetrical budget that delights the fiscal technician could produce pain and suffering for large portions of the population, and neither Dall nor I was willing to settle for that.

So the task of the government budget maker is a complex one. It requires professional precision, command of accounting principles, an ability to work hard under pressure, and a mind and heart that understand the needs of the people as interpreted by the governor and other officials. A budget officer also needs the kind of imagination and resourcefulness that can keep a budget balanced despite lean resources and irrepressible demands for services and tax cuts.

Dall explains all of this in his book and does it very well because he is himself a nice combination of a highly proficient accounting professional and a sensitive and bright student of social needs. The combination is so obviously necessary that I am convinced that the federal model that combines budget making and budget management in the Office of Management and Budget would be desirable for most states as well.

I was extremely fortunate to have Dall as budget director, but he was extremely unfortunate to be available at a time when governors were not surfboard riders. During Dall's tenure, it was a constant struggle to balance the budget without devastating our education and health care institutions or bludgeoning with tax increases those who least could afford them. That we managed to survive the period while doing as much good as we did and without inflicting a lot more pain is a tribute to Dall, the staff, and the others who were working in the agencies.

One cannot read *Memos to the Governor* without being impressed by the extraordinary command he had of the situations he was working in and the options that were available to him. I have only one regret concerning his work: I wish he had written a book like it *before* I became governor instead of after I was elected a private citizen.

Governor Mario M. Cuomo

Preface

The genesis of this book was a course on budgeting that one of us taught for three years at the John F. Kennedy School of Government at Harvard. That course, in turn, drew on our experiences as budget director and chief revenue forecaster in the state of New York, working for Governor Mario M. Cuomo. Our work and study during those years and thereafter persuaded us that the traditional literature on budgeting understated the importance of several critical topics: the influence of the economic cycle on state budgets, the necessity to maintain a long-term strategic perspective in budgeting, and the tactical problem of persuading legislatures to adopt sound budgets. Those themes are recurrent strands in the memos to the governor that follow.

The memo format and the book's title are modeled on Charles L. Schultze's accessible treatise on macroeconomics, *Memos to the President: A Guide through Macroeconomics for the Busy Policymaker* (Brookings Institution Press, 1992). We hope that the use of this format gives these short essays a point of view and directness that more traditional exposition might not convey. For new students of state budgeting, the memo format should help them learn basics of the budget process quickly. The section on budget vocabulary should also help prepare them for more technical material, and the notes highlight a number of the most useful sources of information and articles on state budgeting. More experienced practitioners and scholars should find new points of emphasis, useful examples of good and bad practice, and a practitioner's view of the relationship between governors and their budget directors. Finally, we also hope that from time to time even governors and their advisers will find the memos a useful checklist and reminder of key budget issues and problems. When a state budget director told us that he liked the first edition, we asked him whether he intended to send a copy to his governor. He replied that he preferred not to send the book itself but had passed along the advice in memos under his own name. After some reflection we concluded that this was a compliment.

The personal point of view and informality of the memo format also help to transcend some of the limitations of this book. The format emphasizes the experiential base behind it and makes clear that it is not based on any full-scale and systematic survey of budget practice in all the states. Another limitation is that the book slights budget practices in states that diverge significantly from the norm. In Mississippi, Texas, and South Carolina, for example, where the initial budget proposal is produced by a board or commission rather than by the governor, the process of budget preparation is quite different from the executive budget process described here. In Massachusetts the legislature does not welcome participation by the governor after the executive budget is presented, so the idea of three-way negotiations is foreign to the budget culture of that commonwealth. In every state budget making and adoption will differ in some details from the composite presented here.[1] Nonetheless, elected officials and budgeteers in every state need to consider the central issues emphasized in these memos. They will all profit from developing both a long-term budgetary strategy and a tactical plan for budget adoption, and they will all feel the effects of the business cycle on those strategies and tactics.

This book could not have been written without practical experience drawn from our years of service in the budget office in New York state, so our thanks must go first to Mario Cuomo, who provided that opportunity for service. He would not agree with all the conclusions expressed here, and he might fairly complain that the advice presented in these memos seems much improved by hindsight.

We are also grateful to former colleagues in the New York State Division of the Budget, who are the most capable group of government professionals that we know. We feel very fortunate to have had the opportunity to work with these talented people. Like Cuomo, they would not agree with all of our recommendations.

The students at the Kennedy School helped elaborate some of these ideas, and they and students at the University at Albany provided encouragement and support as these concepts were tested and revised. Barbara Jackson and Allan Clayton-Matthews provided the data in figure 1 in the first edition, and Mark Ibele helped transform those data into a common rate and base series. Dr. Ibele and the California Legislative Analyst's Office provided updated data for the state of California, and Robert Megna of the New York State Division of the Budget directed us to similar data for New York.

At crucial phases in the writing of this book, Brian Roherty and Richard Nathan provided vital encouragement and support. William Keller, Dutch Leonard, Deborah Perry, Martha Roherty, Brian Stenson, and Karen Washabau were generous with their comments on early drafts, and John Collura, Mark Shaw, Dennis Strachota, and two anonymous readers provided helpful suggestions for improvements to later drafts. The second edition also benefited greatly from conversations with Nick Jenny and other researchers at the Rockefeller Institute of Government in Albany, Stacey Mazur at the National Association of Budget Officers, and Robert Kurtter and Renée Boicourt, formerly of Moody's and now with Lamont Financial Services Corporation.

We are also grateful to the Georgetown University Press and its staff for support of this book.

This book is dedicated to our wives and children, who have been never-ending fonts of encouragement and joy. Of course, we alone are responsible for errors of fact or judgment.

Note

1. Edward J. Clynch and Thomas P. Lauth, eds., *Budgeting in the States: Institutions, Processes, and Politics* (Westport, CT: Praeger Publishers, 2006), includes separate essays on budgeting in fifteen different states, including a chapter on New York by the authors of this book. Students of state budgeting can also find useful material about state practices from time to time in *Public Budgeting & Finance,* a quarterly journal featuring articles by practitioners as well as scholars.

Introduction

As a new governor you have a variety of engrossing responsibilities and prerogatives. Among the most important is the central role you now play in formulating the state's budget. As you will discover, your executive budget does not come with an owner's manual, so these memos are designed to help you begin thinking about budget strategy and tactics.

New governors come to office from a variety of backgrounds, with different kinds of experience in budgeting. Some have held legislative posts or run executive-branch agencies. Some bring private-sector experience in financial management. A few have served as elected or appointed finance officers in state or local government. If you are taking office with a limited background in governmental budgeting, these memos will give you a broad overview of the issues and problems you will face in the budget arena. If your background in financial management is more extensive, you might still find this discussion to be a handy checklist and review of the dynamics of statehouse budget making. The heavy emphasis on budget strategy and tactics might also provide some new insight into these vital topics. Whatever your background, the discussion of budgeting and the economic cycle contains important information for political and financial survival.

During your term in office you will spend many long and sometimes painful hours preparing budgets and trying to sell them to the legislature. For the public your success or failure in these activities will be one key factor in forming judgments about your gubernatorial record. Almost by definition, success in budgeting marks a governor as a strong leader, whereas failure in budgeting makes a governor look weak and ineffectual. When the economy slows or slides into recession budget deficits and adoption battles can become chronic ailments, and governors typically find reelection difficult under such circumstances. In the recession of 1990–91 the leading examples were in the northeast, where the economic downturn hit hardest and gap-closing donnybrooks were annual events for many years. As those battles wore on, chief executives, including Governors Madeleine Kunin of Vermont and William O'Neill of Connecticut, chose not to run for reelection. Others, including Governor Michael Dukakis of Massachusetts, were defeated in their reelection bids. Only Mario Cuomo, running against a weak Republican novice and aided by a conservative third-party candidate on the ballot, was reelected. A decade later budget conflict in California, which labored under the largest projected state deficit in history, fueled a successful movement to recall Governor Gray Davis. After the financial crisis of 2008 the economy was an important factor in races for governors in several states. In New Jersey Jon Corzine (D), ex–chief executive officer of Goldman Sachs, ran for reelection in 2009. The economy ranked second to property taxes as a key issue, and Corzine lost by three and a half percentage points to Chris Christie, running as a Republican in a Democratic state. Ohio was severely affected by the economic downturn after the financial crisis. Running for reelection in the fall of 2010, Governor Ted Strickland (D) was opposed by John Kasich, a former member of Congress. According to the Quinnipiac poll: "The economy is the defining issue in the race for governor. Strickland holds an overwhelming 89–6 percent lead among the likely voters who think the economy is improving, but they make up only 19 percent of the electorate. Kasich dominates the 36 percent who think the economy is getting worse 76–13 percent. The 45 percent of voters who think the economy is staying the same back Kasich 50–43 percent."[1] Kasich won the election by a two-point margin.

More substantively, budget success is the key to reorienting government. New programs, changed priorities, tax cuts or shifts in tax burdens, a larger or smaller role for government in the state's economy—all these objectives must be won in the budget arena.

There are no simple definitions of budget success. In these memos a successful budget is one that delivers on a governor's programmatic objectives and does so within financial constraints that help achieve or maintain structural budget balance. Successful budgets are not simply the result of prudent choices in the annual or biennial process of formulating an executive budget.[2] Budget success also requires a clear understanding of the impact of the business cycle on state finances, careful consideration of long-term strategic goals, and effective negotiating tactics to get executive recommendations adopted. These three points will be emphasized again and again in these memos.

Memo 1 discusses your relationship with your budget officer and the kind of skills you should be looking for in that important member of your team. Memo 2, on budget strategy, suggests that you are most likely to achieve your programmatic goals if you fit them into a multiyear budget plan. This memo also reminds you that somewhere in your term in office you are likely to face a recession. You might try to read these two memos first, before getting into the details of budget making.

Memo 3 outlines the approach most budget offices take to budget preparation. This memo is longer and more technical than the other sections, but it will help you understand the framework for your budget choices. Memo 4 discusses the kinds of choices you may face in the late stages of budget preparation.

Memo 5 focuses on the important topic of budget tactics. As you work through the difficult choices that go into your executive budget, you should also be thinking about the legislature and its reaction to your recommendations. Memo 6 discusses your role in presenting the budget to the public, the press, and the legislature.

Memo 7 describes the legislative phase of the budget adoption. Memo 8 discusses the implementation of the budget adopted by the legislature. A final section emphasizes again the importance of your role in laying out a long-term budget strategy and overseeing the tactical plan aimed at passing your executive budget.

Notes

1. www.quinnipiac.edu/x1322.xml?ReleaseID=1520.

2. In 2008 twenty-three states operated under biennial budgets, according to table 1 in *Budget Processes in the States,* published by the National Association of State Budget Officers (Washington, DC: NASBO, 2008). In states with biennial budgets, a two-year version of the multiyear view emphasized below is institutionalized. NASBO publishes this useful survey annually. It can be found, along with other valuable publications, at www .nasbo.org.

MEMO 1

You and Your Budget Officer

Your budget officer is obviously an important factor in the success or failure of your budget strategy. The ideal budget officer brings an imposing set of skills and experience to your administration:

- A background in economics and financial planning deep enough to produce a sophisticated understanding of the state's economy and financial position.
- Sufficient standing and reputation within the community of budget and finance professionals to credibly advance the state's case to the rating agencies and other financially sophisticated audiences.
- The courage to tell the governor the truth about the state's finances.
- The communication skills to explain complex financial issues to a lay public.
- The managerial ability to get the most out of an office staffed by an elite group of state bureaucrats.
- Sufficient knowledge of state agencies and programs to ensure fair and complete presentation of the policy implications of budget options.
- The political savvy to help map out a strategy for budget adoption.
- The negotiating skills, patience, and experience for working with legislative counterparts to produce a final budget.

As you might guess, finding one person who fills this description is for all practical purposes impossible. Instead of looking for superheroes, chief executives typically try other approaches, most of them aimed at building a strong team in the budget office whose members possess most of these capacities. In staffing the US Office of Management and Budget (OMB), for example, President Bill Clinton initially paired Leon Panetta, a seasoned legislator, with Alice Rivlin, an economist who won the respect of the financial and policymaking communities during her tenure as the head of the Congressional Budget Office.

In many states governors select a budget or finance officer with strong political skills, counting on the professionalism of the permanent staff in the budget office to provide the necessary technical capabilities. In Connecticut Governor Lowell Weicker acted quickly after his election in November of 1990 to appoint William Cibes, a college professor and former state legislator who had served as chair of the Ways and Means Committee, to run his Office of Policy and Management. Cibes's political background and his broad experience in state budgetary matters were important elements in Weicker's successful battle to enact an income tax. In early 2010 Governor Chris Christie chose a former New York City Council member as treasurer of New Jersey. And in New York in 1998 Governor Pataki chose Bob King, a former elected county executive, to be his budget director.

In other states—including Florida, Massachusetts, Minnesota, and New Jersey—the budget officer reports to a cabinet-level officer with wider responsibilities.[1] Although this arrangement distances the budget office from the governor, it also allows the governor to supplement the skills of the budget director with whatever different capabilities the cabinet officer possesses.

In New York, where the director of the budget division is a cabinet-level position, each of Governor Mario Cuomo's budget directors had previously served as first deputy in the budget office. By using this approach Cuomo guaranteed continuity and ensured that the director had detailed knowledge about the budget and the budget office. Cuomo also inserted members of his own staff into budget making to add political sensitivity and communications skills as needed. His son, Governor Andrew Cuomo, continued this tradition by reappointing his predecessor's budget director, Bob Megna, to lead the budget office soon after taking office in January 2011. Governor Cuomo also brought back to Albany several key advisers from his term as attorney general, as well as former advisers to his father. In California Governor Jerry Brown reappointed his predecessor's budget director, Ana Matosantos, who was the state's youngest budget director and first Latina budget director in December 2010, before being sworn in as governor.[2]

Whatever the background and skills of the person you appoint, you should expect that from time to time your budget officer will bring you unpleasant news. Although the precipitating cause will vary, the following types of events are common sources of bad news.

Economic Slowdown and the Business Cycle

Several times in these memos you will be reminded of the powerful impact of the business cycle in budgeting. The American economy alternates between periods of growth and recessions. These national cycles will also affect the economy in your state, and you will feel the impact in economically sensitive revenue sources, such as sales and income taxes. Indeed, these revenue sources often rise and fall more than the indicators of economic growth. The economy of your state is also affected by regional forces, usually reflecting changes in the prospects of the industries of most importance in that region. These regional forces, which will also have a powerful impact on your state's finances, are notoriously difficult to predict. Sometime during your term in office it is likely that you will experience firsthand the effects of a recession on your state's budget. The earliest warning of that event will probably come from your budget officer, notifying you that revenues are falling short of estimates.

Forecasting Errors

Budgets are based on hundreds of different estimates and forecasts. Good management can make some of those predictions come true. For example, careful control of hiring and salaries can guarantee that you will not overrun the budget estimate for your own gubernatorial staff. Many other events of importance to your budget are not subject to managerial control. For example, estimates of all major revenues, forecasts of welfare caseloads, health care inflation estimates, and a host of other forecasts all reflect forces and events that you and your top managers can do little to control. At the core of those estimates are forecasts of the state's economy and demography, and those forecasts can be wrong, sometimes for several years in a row.

By its nature budgeting is an error-prone activity. These errors do not necessarily reflect a lack of technical capability or failure of effort on the part of your budget staff. Forecasts can be simply wrong, and from time to time your budget officer will bring you news of those errors. We will return to this topic in a discussion of risk and revenue.

Program or Managerial Failures

The budget office considers, however briefly, every program in every agency as it puts together its recommendations for you. The budget office also tracks spending in every agency as the operating budget is executed during the current fiscal year. As one of the few officials with this broad, government-wide perspective, your budget officer regularly receives reports from budget staffers about agency management and program performance. Because not all managers and programs will perform well, you will sometimes hear bad news from the budget director about your other appointees or your programmatic initiatives.

Although both you and your budget officer will find this role of bearing bad news tiresome, you must deal with these grim episodes in a way that does not choke off these difficult but important communications. Governors need people around them who are prepared to speak truth to power, and by position and training your budget officer is expected to play that role.[3] The alternative, which is even more tiresome, is to learn about these problems, errors, and failures in the media, without the early warning you can get from your budget officer and other top staff. If none of your staff brings you bad news, it does not mean nothing bad is happening in your government or in the state. It means no one around you is willing to deliver the message when things go wrong.

You will get early and confidential briefings about bad news in the state's finances from your budget officer. You should understand, however, that events, especially trips to the bond or note markets, will require you or the budget director to share those facts with the rest of the world. Since New York City's fiscal crisis in the mid-1970s officials of state and local governments have been legally mandated to make full and timely disclosure about their governments' finances in official documents used to market notes and bonds. The Securities and Exchange Commission (SEC) also requires what it calls continuing disclosure—that is, speedy public notice of negative financial news even when a government is not marketing its securities. These and other regulations make it difficult to manage the release of bad news about the state's finances the way you might manage news of other problems. Please remind your press officer that the culprit is the SEC, not your budget director. Two examples may help make the point. In May 1987 New York had to make an unexpected amendment to its official statement shortly before a multibillion-dollar cash flow borrowing. The disclosure revealed that tax returns filed weeks earlier were coming up significantly short in the wake of a dramatic federal tax reform that took effect in the 1986 tax year.[4] More recently Governor Christie in New Jersey announced a surprise budget deficit in early 2010, shortly after the state issued transportation bonds, and this deficit also required an amendment to disclosure documents.[5] Bond investors prefer to receive bad news before they buy bonds rather than afterward.

In light of these and other pressures you may discover that budget directors sometimes do not stay in the job as long as you might like. You will find this turnover easier to handle if you and the director begin to think about grooming a successor long before you expect your incumbent director to leave. Indeed, if you are reelected more than once, you are likely to outlast the vast majority of your top managers and assistants. The question of managerial succession is always an important topic, and prudent chief executives in government, like their counterparts in the corporate world, plan for personnel shifts before they are faced with vacancies that are unexpected and unwelcome.

Budget offices also serve nonfinancial functions for the chief executive. As its name suggests, the OMB performs some managerial and policy functions, and many states and localities have also broadened the base of activities performed by the budget office. Our own view, which is not universally held, is that it makes sense for a governor to ask his financial managers to concentrate on their financial functions and then set up other staff agencies or special groups to perform project management and other nonfinancial activities. We believe that state budget officers will serve their governors better by avoiding the OMB path and broadening their roles into full-fledged chief financial officers. Thus, these memos concentrate on the budget officer as financial manager and budget strategist and tactician, a narrowly drawn but demanding set of roles.

Notes

1. See NASBO, *Budget Processes in the States* (2008), table 3, for data on who appoints the budget director.

2. For many years the top ranks of state budget offices were hostile environments for women. Since the early 1990s, however, women have

distinguished themselves as budget directors in many states, such as Alaska, California, Florida, Hawaii, Kentucky, Maine, Massachusetts, Michigan, Minnesota, Missouri, New York, and Virginia. African American and Latino budget professionals remain underrepresented in top budget jobs.

3. Aaron B. Wildavsky used this phrase in the title of his text on policy analysis, *Speaking Truth to Power: The Art and Craft of Policy Analysis* (New Brunswick, NJ: Transaction Books, 1987). The Quakers stake out an earlier claim, however, tracing the phrase to a charge given to eighteenth-century Friends. See "Speak Truth to Power: A Quaker Search for an Alternative to Violence," a pamphlet prepared by the American Friends Service Committee in 1955.

4. This was referred to as *stickering* the official statement because underwriters placed a sticker with new text on the front page of the document.

5. Lisa Fleisher, "N.J.'s Deficit, Budget Updates Could Impact Market, Investors Say, January 28, 2010," NorthJersey.com, www.northjersey .com/news/012810_NJs_deficit_budget_updates_could_impact_market_ investors_say.html.

MEMO 2

Budget Strategy

While you were running for office you made speeches and issued position papers with budget implications. These public statements and promises may have been very narrow and specific—new programs for special constituencies, for example—or you may have laid out much broader objectives about shrinking or expanding the role of state government. The job of your budget director is to formulate a long-term plan to achieve those objectives and still keep the state's budget in balance.

During your campaign you may not have been fully knowledgeable about the state's financial position. Moreover, you may not have had a clear sense of the full cost of your proposals to increase services, fund new projects or programs, or cut taxes. Early efforts at developing a strategic plan that matches your objectives with the state's resources can be painful and may require some changes in your goals or the timetable for putting your plans into effect. While campaigning for governor of North Carolina, candidate Bev Perdue said in fall 2008, "I don't believe you can raise taxes in an economy with folks struggling the way they are." However, Governor Perdue signed a $1 billion tax increase in early 2009, including a one-cent increase in the state sales tax.[1]

The rest of this memo discusses the elements of a strategic budget plan and outlines the fiscal constraints within which such a plan must be implemented. As you will see, the managerial problem of maintaining budget balance over several years adds a level of complexity to choices you will face in any single budget.

Policy Objectives

Few politicians get elected without making campaign promises, some of which reflect their strongly held views about how they would like to change government programs or priorities. A useful first step in developing a strategic budget plan is simply to list the objectives that you and your staff believe will have an impact on state budgets, together with appropriate excerpts from speeches or issue papers in which the proposals were presented. Some of those proposals will include very specific promises to

- create new programs;
- add to existing programs;
- build or repair capital facilities around the state; and
- cut specific taxes.

More broadly, you may have pledged to avoid tax increases, shrink the scope of government, reduce the growth of budgets, or reduce state borrowing. Furthermore, you may have other specific or general ideas about new directions for state government beyond those contained in your public statements. Your budget officer needs a full understanding of your views on these issues to outline a strategic budget plan for your term in office.

The time between your election and the presentation of your first budget will be short. You may find it difficult to make a comprehensive listing of your objectives. Your budget officer may be much more comfortable thinking about the annual budget and may find it difficult to sketch out a multiyear picture of the state's finances. Nonetheless, it is important for you to take the time to discuss strategic goals and to understand the state's long-term fiscal position before you move on to detailed discussion of the upcoming executive budget. If you and your budget officer have not agreed on a broad strategic plan, your first budget is likely to create as many problems as it solves. For example, you may find that the budget does not provide a credible down payment on your most critical programmatic objectives. Alternatively, your plans and proposals may be fully incorporated, but the budget may be funded in ways that will undermine the state's fiscal position during the next few years of your term.

This first fiscal year is critical. You will want to evaluate carefully the potential benefits of an austere budget before you own the consequences of past decisions and determine whether that approach might provide a foundation for initiatives that can be put in place before you run for reelection.

Financial Objectives

At the same time that you are compiling a list of your promises and objectives, the budget staff will be preparing briefings for you on the state's economic and fiscal position. An important norm of the professional staff in budget offices is loyalty to the chief executive. Regardless of whether they voted for you, the staff in your budget office will be working hard, often in the evening and on weekends, to achieve your stated objectives. They are also bound, usually by law and always by professional ethics, to maintain budget balance as they implement your objectives.

As we will soon see, budget balance is not a simple concept. However it is defined, the constraints that affect state budgets are very real. As Presidents Ronald Reagan and George W. Bush learned early on, it is impossible to increase spending on major programs (defense, for instance), cut taxes, *and* balance the budget. In both cases the goal of a balanced budget was soon abandoned. For the federal government a balanced budget is a worthy goal in good economic times but not a legal requirement. Traditionally when presidents do not balance the federal budget, the immediate consequences are minor, but in August 2011 Standard & Poor's downgraded US long-term debt from AAA to AA+ out of concern that legislative dysfunction would make it very difficult for the federal government to rein in budget deficits over the longer term.

The situation is different for governors. In forty-eight states some sort of balanced budget requirement is in effect.[2] Moreover, chronic budget deficits do lead to downgrades in state credit ratings. Though no one, not even a fiscal officer, should argue that credit ratings are inviolable, they are important and highly visible measures of the state's fiscal health, and lower ratings increase the costs of borrowing. Downgrades in credit ratings can also have political consequences. Challengers to sitting governors can and do use downgrades as evidence for their charges of fiscal mismanagement.

In short your budget officer will be trying to keep your promises and keep your budget balanced. If you have promised to raise spending and cut taxes, your budget officer will not present you with options that unbalance your budget. Instead, the budget director will come back to you with a plan calling for cuts in the spending areas where you have not promised to spend more, revenue increases in areas where you have not pledged to cut taxes, or both. If you find those gap-closing steps unpalatable, the plan might have to be altered to postpone or eliminate implementation of less important objectives.

A third alternative is to move ahead full speed to implement your objectives and balance your first annual budget with nonrecurring actions, more colloquially known as *one-shots* and sometimes tagged as *gimmicks*. As detailed below, this option will be tempting, but a budget built on nonrecurring actions is likely to cause you serious problems later in your term. This is why these memos stress the importance of a multiyear plan that will make those dynamics evident and help you grasp the complex concept of structural budget balance.[3]

Structural Budget Balance

A budget is balanced when spending and revenues are equal.[4] The balanced-budget concept becomes more complex, however, when you extend your planning horizon for more than one year.

In a multiyear plan it is important to distinguish between *recurring* and *nonrecurring* spending and revenues.

If the goal is simply to balance the budget in any single year, you will choose from actions that increase revenues or cut spending during that period. Some of those gap-closing actions may have permanent impacts. For instance, enacting a new tax will create a stream of revenues over the long term, and eliminating a spending program provides continuing savings. Other steps may help close the gap during the budget year but provide no recurring benefit. Examples include a delay in the phase-in of a new program, which will save money, but only until the program is fully implemented; the sale of state assets, which provides nonrecurring revenue; or a speedup in tax collections, which provides a one-time benefit. It is even possible to reduce spending in the current year by steps that increase spending in later years. A simple example is issuing bonds instead of using tax revenues to pay for a capital project. The tax revenues will be available for other purposes, including closing a budget gap, but future budgets must include principal and interest payments on those bonds.

If you extend your time horizon to think about budget balance over a multiyear period, nonrecurring actions become much less attractive, because the gaps they fill temporarily will return in the very next budget period. The use of nonrecurring savings or revenues in one year to finance recurring spending—prison costs or school aid, for example—leaves a hole in future budgets. And if those recurring costs are growing—and most state programs do grow in cost—the hole in future budgets will be even larger than the gap you struggled to fill originally. As suggested earlier, these chronic budget problems can weaken a governor's political standing and sap time and attention that you might prefer to devote to more productive activities.

To avoid creating this continuing fiscal stress, you should think of budget balance more broadly, aiming to balance recurring spending with recurring revenues. If you can maintain this balance between recurring revenues and spending over a multiyear period, your budget is in structural balance.

It is easier to describe this happy result than to achieve it. To put it simply, spending usually increases more quickly than revenues. Even without deliberate action to expand programs, state spending grows for a variety of reasons. In recent years, some of the more important sources of spending growth have included inflation in the health care sector, cost pressures in all sectors of education, and pay raises for state workers. Similarly, state revenues grow even without tax increases when the economic activity being taxed expands or when inflation leads to higher incomes or prices. Unfortunately, there is no reason to expect spending and revenues to grow at the same rate. In recent years, recurring spending has grown significantly faster in most states than existing revenues, especially in program areas such as corrections and Medicaid.[5] As a result, governors and legislators have had to increase revenues and reduce spending growth simply to sustain structural budget balance, fighting hard just to stay even.

The Business Cycle and Budget Balance

Built-in spending growth is one reason why governments find it difficult to sustain structural balance. A second and less predictable complication is the business cycle. As mentioned earlier, the economy in the United States grows unevenly, with periods of expansion followed by periods of contraction, called recessions; a lay definition of a recession is a contraction or decline in the economy that lasts for more than two calendar quarters.[6] Economists and policymakers have not been able to predict with any certainty the timing or duration of recessions, and their incidence has varied widely.

The ups and downs of the business cycle create a treacherous environment for budgeting. Figure 2.1 depicts the growth rate for tax receipts from a large state across a period that includes the complete cycle of growth and recession.[7] The shaded

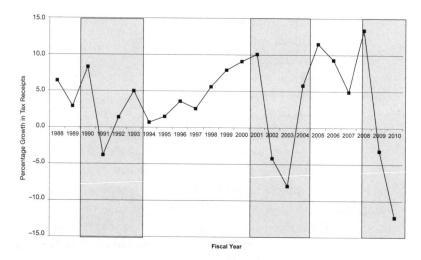

Figure 2.1.   Percentage Growth in Tax Receipts.

portions represent recession periods in that state. As you might expect, economically sensitive revenue sources, such as sales and income taxes, grow more quickly during economic expansion than in recession. History notwithstanding, government policy-makers tend to assume that the higher levels of revenue growth in the expansion phase will be permanent and use those grow-ing revenues to pay for continuing programs or to make per-manent cuts in taxes. When the next recession comes—and it always does—these policymakers are forced to increase taxes or make sharp cuts in spending to balance their budgets each year. Alternatively, government officials resort to nonrecurring actions to close their annual budget gaps and, in doing so, run the risk of several years of structurally unbalanced budgets and the chronic fiscal stress they create.

To avoid this painful condition, policymakers need to re-member that some portion of the revenue growth during the expansion phase of the economy is itself nonrecurring—a *cyclical surplus,* if you will. If government officials set some of the cyclical surpluses aside in reserves and avoid using those revenues to pay for continuing programs or permanent tax cuts, budget balancing during recessions will be a much less difficult task. Because economists cannot precisely predict the ups and downs of the business cycle, the management of these cyclical surpluses and deficits is not an exact science. But we can be sure that it will be easier to maintain structural balance, and easier to avoid damaging tax increases and layoffs in the midst of recessions, if policymakers avoid excessive program increases and permanent tax cuts during the growth period of the economic cycle.

Some governors have persuaded legislators to establish reserve funds as cushions against the vicissitudes of the business cycle. Popularly labeled rainy-day funds, these reserves have different titles in different states. A governor may decide that it is simply too difficult to persuade the legislature to maintain reserves such as rainy-day funds when those funds could be used for immediate spending on programs and projects. Indeed, for legislators, the rainy day may be the next election. A budget without reserves, however, is subject to much more stress when the business cycle turns down, and you are likely to find that some additional protection during a recession is worth the tactical problem of persuading legislators that state government needs to bolster its reserves. Adequate reserves will also strengthen your case with the rating agencies.

The National Association of State Budget Officers (NASBO) maintains data on one crude measure of how well states are prepared for economic downturn. NASBO tracks what it calls total year-end balances, consisting of rainy-day funds, other explicit reserves, and year-end surpluses or deficits in the general fund. As figure 2.2 shows, the states as a group do indeed increase year-end balances during good times and draw them down during recessions. Indeed, after the recession of 1990–91, states built those balances up to 10.4 percent, the highest level since NASBO started tracking the measure. These reserves helped cushion state budgets when recession hit at the turn of the

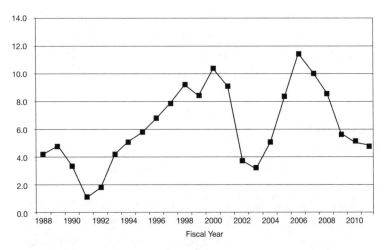

Figure 2.2.   Preparing for Recession: Total Year-End Balances as a Percentage of State Expenditures.

century, but two years later estimated balances had been drawn down to 1.3 percent, and state governments were still suffering through significant fiscal stress. States repeated this pattern in the run-up to the 2007 recession, hitting a high of 11.5 percent, before drawing reserves down to 4.9 percent over the next three years.[8]

Budget Strategy—A Summary

Before building your first annual budget, you should outline your programmatic and budgetary priorities and sit down with your budget director to work out a long-term strategy to achieve those objectives. Ideally, that plan will outline a strategy for the next four years. One important factor in this strategic plan will be where the state stands in the business cycle. Another key factor will be whether your predecessor has left you a structurally balanced budget or a chronic structural deficit.

As you consider your long-term budget prospects, you may find that you will have to cut spending more deeply than you might have hoped or advocate tax increases that you had hoped to avoid. You might also find it necessary to cut back or slow down implementation of some of your initiatives. You will certainly be tempted to use nonrecurring actions to avoid these unpleasant alternatives. Before you do so, be certain that you understand the long-term implications of those temporary gap-closers. Many governors have found that this supposed solution for their budget problem has left them with chronic structural deficits and the political and governmental strains that attend that condition. In short, the so-called cure can produce a lingering and debilitating illness.

The economy will change, often unpredictably, and your long-term plans will also change. Thus, you should repeat this strategic budget review every year, pushing the planning period out another year, before embarking on detailed decision making for the executive budget. As your term proceeds you will naturally focus more intensely on the year in which you might run for reelection. If possible, you will want your major programmatic objectives under way by then. But equally important, you will want to go into that year with your budget solidly balanced, backed by reserves sufficient to handle an unexpected economic slowdown. Your worst budget nightmare is a recession in an election year, with the attendant disruption it can cause—legislative stalemate, cutbacks in key programs and aid to schools and localities, layoffs, tax increases, and rating downgrades, to name the most obvious symptoms. No strategy can completely protect you against all economic contingencies, but a structurally balanced budget with adequate reserves can give you time and resources to respond more deliberately in an economic downturn.

You may find it difficult to maintain a four-year strategic perspective when you are only a year or so from your own election date. Nevertheless, making the effort is worthwhile. Thinking about the budget you will have to manage when your second term begins can help ward off some of the pressures to stretch the election-year budget beyond reasonable fiscal limits.

Notes

1. For a proposed sin tax increase see www.governor.state.nc.us/News Items/PressReleaseDetail.aspx?newsItemID=213, and for the later proposed sales tax increase see hwww.governor.state.nc.us/NewsItems/Uploaded Files/8be52414-c6f4-46a3-907b-f79b92cdc240.pdf; also see Balfour, Brian, Bev Purdue's Broken Campaign Promises, blog post April 27, 2010, www.nccivitas.org/2010/bev-purdue-s-broken-campaign-promises/.

2. In all but six states there is a statutory or constitutional requirement for the governor to submit a balanced executive budget. In three of the six the legislature is required to enact a balanced budget, and in a fourth the governor is required to execute a budget where actual revenues are equal to spending. Only Indiana and Vermont lack some kind of requirement for budget balance, although in Vermont, at least, this does not appear to be a practical issue since the state does not carry deficits forward to future years. (See NASBO, *Budget Processes in the States* [2008], table 11.)

3. Allen J. Proctor and his staff at the New York State Financial Control Board made an impressive effort to operationalize the concept of structural balance in several reports, especially *Structural Balance* (New York: Financial Control Board, 1992).

4. In the finance statutes that required balanced budgets these terms are not defined as consistently as they are in the private sector. For example, revenue is generally measured on a cash basis and can include temporary resources and cash borrowed from future years—resources that will not always count as revenue under generally accepted accounting principles.

5. The Governmental Accountability Office has modeled the very long-term outlook for the state-local sector as a whole in several recent reports. The agency concludes that to maintain balance over the longer term the state-local sector would have to make cuts in current expenditures of about 12.5 percent or raise taxes by an equivalent amount. It notes that "the primary driver of long-term fiscal challenges for the state and local government sector continues to be the projected growth in health-related costs. Specifically, state and local expenditures on Medicaid and the cost of health insurance for state and local retirees and employees are projected to grow more than GDP." (See Governmental Accountability Office, *State and Local Governments' Fiscal Outlook*, April 2011 Update, Report GAO-11-495SP.)

6. The National Bureau of Economic Research is the official arbiter of recessions and sometimes will declare a recession even if the downturn has not lasted two quarters.

7. These data are for major tax revenues collected by the state of New York, adjusted to be comparable over time. In this kind of counterfactual

data series, historical data are adjusted upward or downward to reflect what collections might have been under current tax rates and bases. No attempt is made to estimate dynamic changes, such as the reductions in demand that would be caused by higher sales taxes. This series was compiled by the New York State Budget Division and was published on page 10 of the *Economic and Revenue Outlook, Executive Budget FY 2012*. This document is available at http://www.budget.ny.us/pubs/archive/fy1112archiveBudget 1112/economicRevenueOutlook/economicRevenueOutlook.pdf.

8. See table 28, *Fiscal Survey of the States Spring 2011* (Washington, DC: NASBO, 2011) for data on total year-end balances. This important survey is published each fall by NASBO and the National Governors Association. The data point for 2011 is a NASBO estimate. The data for earlier years are actuals.

MEMO 3

Preparing the Executive Budget—
The Technical Underpinnings

Each year (or two, if your state has a biennial budget) you will send the legislature your spending and revenue recommendations. In the pages that follow you will see how this executive budget proposal is constructed and get a preview of your role in its preparation and presentation. By the end of this section you should understand the dynamics of the budget-making process and have some familiarity with the technical terms used in budgeting. If you have time, please read the section called "Budget Vocabulary" at the end of this volume. Because fiscal terminology varies slightly from state to state, you should ask the budget office for a glossary describing the special vocabulary used for budgeting in your state. They are often published as appendixes to the annual budget.

Throughout the budget process you will be the recipient of memoranda, charts, tables, and lists. Most will be filled with numbers, sometimes with little guidance on the origins of those calculations. Between the numbers and the jargon, these documents can seem forbidding at best and indecipherable at worst. Please complain when the presentations are not clear. It is the job of the top staffers in the budget office to make their recommendations to you in a format that you can understand. They cannot succeed at this task unless you tell them when they have failed to be comprehensible. As they reformat their presentations to make better sense to you and as you become more familiar with the budget process and jargon, you will find that budget data and documents become much less mysterious.

The Budget Process and Calendar

The budgetary process can be divided into three main phases:

- *Preparation:* With input from operating agencies, program staff, and special task forces, the budget office prepares recommendations for the executive budget. After the governor and his or her staff review and modify those recommendations, the budget is presented to the legislature and the public.
- *Adoption:* The legislature reviews the budget, makes changes, and votes to enact the budget, usually by a majority vote. Some states require a supermajority to adopt the budget. For example, Rhode Island's constitution requires a two-thirds majority of elected members in each house to pass appropriation bills. In most states the governor can make further changes after adoption through a line-item veto.[1]
- *Execution:* As the new fiscal year begins, usually on July 1, the adopted budget is put into effect.[2] With oversight from the budget office, agencies implement spending cuts or new programs, aid payments are made under revised formulae, and changes in taxes take effect. During the year the budget office monitors spending and tax collections and recommends modifications in the budget if necessary.

The preparation phase of the budget is the subject of this memo. We will discuss adoption and execution in more detail later. For now it is important to note that you, your budget officer, and other key advisers must be thinking about the legislative response to the executive budget throughout its preparation, just as the coach of a football team considers the reactions of the other team in preparing a game plan. Indeed, your choice of tactics will sometimes dictate your decision about a spending or revenue option or your judgment about how conservative your revenue estimates should be. We will return to this question of budget tactics in the next memo.

Counting backward from the statutory presentation dates for the budget and for your state-of-the-state address, the budget office will create a detailed calendar, laying out the deadlines for the many steps in budget making. You and your scheduler should sit down as soon as possible after you receive this schedule to make sure that time is blocked out for your detailed review of budget recommendations. The time commitment can be substantial. By one account, California governors spend five hours a day for two weeks during December on budget review.[3]

The Fundamental Constraint—The State's Economy

The first step in the budgetary process is an early estimate of the economic climate in the state and the revenue growth that existing tax sources will produce at current rates. These estimates typically form the basis of a communication from the budget office to the agencies, sometimes labeled *budget guidelines* or a *call letter*, outlining the fiscal situation faced by the state and detailing how agency budget data and programmatic proposals are submitted to the budget office. As you take office, this early estimate will be updated with more recent economic data and presented to you in a memo outlining broadly the budgetary framework in which the rest of the preparation phase will take place. Like all forecasts, this one will be wrong in some respects and will be updated again as budget preparation draws to a close.

The economy of the state is the source of government's revenue. Individuals and corporations pay taxes or fees based on some kind of economic activity—wages and salaries earned, purchases of goods or services, corporate profits, and so forth. In the short run state government can do little to increase the level of economic activity that it taxes. Thus, the level of economic activity in the state is a very real constraint within which budget making must take place.

In your work as governor you will face other constraints, many of which your own efforts can overcome. Legislators and editorial writers can be persuaded to change their minds. Citizens can be swayed by your rhetoric. Better management can improve the productivity of state workers. But neither persuasion nor rhetoric nor management will increase the economic base that supports state tax revenues in the next fiscal year. Within the limits of forecasting technology, the goal of your budget officer will be to provide a realistic and unbiased picture of the state's economy as input into the budget-making process.[4]

Revenue Estimates

A forecast of the national economy is the initial statistical underpinning of the revenue side of the budget. Because there is little reason to believe that the state workers who prepare these forecasts understand the national economy better than the rest of the community of professional economists, the budget office's national forecast is usually based on projections prepared by one of a handful of firms that maintain complex mathematical models of the US economy. These corporations update their projections regularly, taking into account the changing dynamics of the national economy as well as the frequent revisions in economic statistics produced by the relevant federal agencies. When the credit-rating agencies evaluate your budget, they will expect the state's forecast of the national economy to be consistent with the forecasts made by those firms and with the consensus of forecasts of nationally known economists, whose projections are summarized in a newsletter called *Blue Chip Economic Indicators*. From time to time the *Wall Street Journal* also publishes a summary of economic forecasts, and the Congressional Budget

Office regularly updates its detailed economic forecast, which also serves as a useful benchmark.

The next step is preparation of an economic forecast for the state's own economy. Forecasters in the budget office consult with economists from local banks, utilities, the appropriate Federal Reserve banks, and universities to help develop that state forecast. They may also use data from the economic consulting firms mentioned above. The relationship between the national and state economies is especially difficult to predict. In recent decades some regions have found themselves mired in recessions while the national economy was growing. In the 1980s cyclical downturns moved through several regions, hitting the farm belt, the oil patch, and the rust belt. By 1988 the economy of New England, which had outperformed the nation for nearly a decade, lost its economic strength, and the Northeast suffered through a recession much deeper and longer than the rest of the country. In 1994 the California economy was still deeply troubled while the economy of the United States continued to grow. By 1996 growth in the California economy was once again outpacing the nation, only to be hit by energy shortages and the dot-com collapse as the new century began. The 2007 recession was triggered in part by a huge housing price bust that followed an extraordinary run-up in prices. Although the bust touched every region, it was much more severe in some states than others, most notably Arizona, California, Florida, and Nevada. As a consequence these states' economies were harder hit than most other states.

Economists know less about regional trends and cycles than they do about the national economy. Consequently, changes in these trends, such as those that affected the Northeast in the 1980s and the housing-bust states more recently, are notoriously difficult to predict. Your revenue estimators will keep in touch with their counterparts in other states and with economists who have regional perspectives. Beyond that, the best that you and your staff can do is watch with great care the industries that dominate your state's economy as well as the smaller but more volatile sectors—construction, finance, or technology, for example—that can overheat and collapse. Changes in these key sectors may provide clues to shifts in the linkage between the state and national economies. The rating agencies will expect the state economic forecast used in the executive budget to be consistent with forecasts and activity in neighboring states, except where your staff have good reasons for differences.

With national and state economic forecasts in hand, forecasters can produce estimates of the revenues expected from each major tax source at current rates. If budgeting is an error-prone activity, incorrect revenue estimates are the most visible kinds of error. Forecasters must base their projections on state and national economic forecasts, which are bound to be wrong in some respects. Forecasters must work with economic data that are frequently revised and with tax collection data that can be difficult to interpret. Moreover, taxpayer behavior also changes, usually in response to changes in the federal tax code. In the best of times revenue forecasts can be off by as much as 2 percent. When national tax laws or economic trends are changing, much larger errors are not uncommon. In 2009, the year in which the recent recession hit state finances the hardest, the median state overestimated the combined revenue from the personal income tax, the sales tax, and corporate income tax by 10.2 percent.[5]

Although the estimate for each tax is subject to significant risk, forecasters try to keep their estimates balanced so that the aggregate estimate for total tax revenues is likely to be less volatile. If the strategy works, one or more revenue sources may come in higher than estimated, offsetting in part other errors on the downside. If the estimates are unbiased and risks are evenly distributed, the state may still hit its overall revenue target, even if estimates for individual taxes are wrong. Unfortunately, when the economy turns down, it is not uncommon to see significant shortfalls in all economically sensitive taxes.

With all of these sources of error, you might wonder why your own views should not weigh heavily in the revenue-estimating process. In fact, the budget director will want to know how much risk you are willing to tolerate as revenue estimates and other important projections are reviewed. As you might expect, the budget office is likely to come down in favor of conservative estimates. Risk tolerance is a complex issue, however, and your decision will depend on several factors, including the position of the economy in the business cycle, the level of reserves held by the state, and the state's credit rating. If the concept of risk tolerance seems overly abstract, ask yourself a more practical question—how much protection would you like against budget shortfalls during the upcoming fiscal year?

As suggested in the next memo, which discusses legislative negotiations, you may sometimes decide that it makes sense to adjust your risk exposure for tactical purposes. For example, you may ask your budget director to use very conservative revenue estimates in your executive budget. If the economy does not deteriorate, you might be able to raise those projections at the end of legislative negotiations to pay for additional spending or tax cuts proposed by the legislature. Tactical decisions of this kind sometimes work as planned and sometimes backfire. In this example, slower-than-expected economic growth could wipe out any planned increase in estimates.

Although your overall risk tolerance is an important guideline for budget making, it is dangerous for you or your top staff to tinker with individual revenue estimates. Several kinds of problems may result. First, unless you are a professional economist, your intervention will not be based on better information about the state's real economic activity but will reflect your wishes and hopes that revenues might be higher, making your budget-balancing chore easier. But wishing for higher revenues will not produce additional cash, which can be generated only by additional economic activity or higher tax rates. Second, your budget officer must defend the budget's revenue estimates before the credit-rating agencies and the rest of the financial community. To be defensible those estimates must be internally consistent and in line with expectations in neighboring states. Finally, tinkering with revenue estimates creates a dangerous dynamic in the relationship between you and your budget officer. Anticipating that you will push estimates higher, the budget office may trim back its initial projections to make room for your intervention. When that happens, your fears that your budget office might be deliberately underestimating revenues will be substantiated. This kind of gamesmanship leads to distrust and confusion and is not likely to produce what you need most—realistic and unbiased advice from your budget officer about the revenues that you can expect during the next budget period.

The Spending Baseline

While revenue forecasters are estimating how much revenue will be available in the next fiscal year, other professionals in the budget office are working on the spending side of the budget. The budget staffers who oversee programs and agencies comb through their spending plans, preparing recommendations for the upcoming fiscal year. In a few areas the estimating process will resemble revenue forecasting—that is, the budget staffers (often called budget examiners) will be trying to project the impact of economic and demographic trends on state spending. To estimate welfare costs, for example, budget examiners will prepare statistical forecasts of the cash assistance caseload, based on previous levels of cases, population trends, and estimates of unemployment rates. The caseload data, in combination with statutory benefit levels, will produce a spending total for the cash-assistance portion of welfare spending.

More frequently, however, the output of a budget examiner's work is not a statistical forecast but, rather, a construct peculiar to budgeting called a *spending baseline*. The baseline is usually designed to estimate how much it will cost to continue the level of agency or program services at next year's prices for labor and materials. This *current-services baseline*, sometimes called the *continuation budget*, is a powerful concept in budgeting, and you need to understand its operation. The term *construct* is used here in discussing the spending baseline to emphasize the differences between this activity and the more familiar forecasting discussed above. From your point of view the baseline will be the starting point for a series of choices you will make about state spending, not a statistical projection of how much money the state will spend next year. These distinctions should become clearer as you complete this memo. You might, however, ask your budget officer to go over in more detail the methodology for constructing spending baselines in your state, because practice and terminology vary somewhat from jurisdiction to jurisdiction.

Current Services

In an agency with a stable workforce and workload, the calculation of next year's spending baseline is straightforward. The budget examiner begins with the staffing level at the time budget preparation begins. Salaries for personnel are adjusted upward from the current year's level by collective-bargaining increases and other relevant factors, such as mandated longevity increments. That adjusted salary, multiplied by the current staffing level, will be the agency's baseline personnel budget. Similarly, the current budget for various categories of supplies and materials will be adjusted upward by the appropriate inflation factors. For example, a budget allocation for office supplies might be increased by 3 percent and spending for fuel might be adjusted by a higher or lower factor, based on economic models available to the budget office. Finally, the budget will be adjusted downward to eliminate any one-time allocations in the current year's budget—to purchase office furniture or new equipment, for example—because the baseline is supposed to reflect only recurring costs.

Constructing the baseline is more complex for an agency with a growing workforce. Assume, for example, that the current year's budget has authorized a new internal auditing agency, which will eventually have a staff of thirty. As the fiscal year begins staff on board may be much smaller. With additional hiring occurring throughout the year, the agency may not reach its full head count until the end of the year, and it certainly will not need to budget for salaries an amount sufficient to pay for all thirty workers for the full year.

As budget making begins in the fall the agency may have hired half of its authorized total. If the budget examiner uses the current staffing of fifteen to calculate next year's baseline budget, the audit group will never have enough funding to hire its full complement of employees. In these circumstances the budget examiner will construct a baseline for the next fiscal year, using the full authorized staffing of thirty and will allow full-year salaries for those workers. (*Annualization* of this year's budget is the technician's term for these calculations.) Similarly, allocations for supplies and materials will be increased by an inflation factor, but they will also be adjusted upward so the base budget fully reflects the costs of the growing head count.

In an agency with a shrinking workforce the process is reversed. The examiner will delete unneeded funding to be sure that the agency has only enough funding to pay for next year's smaller head count and to shrink allocations for materials, equipment, and other needs accordingly.

After budget examiners have constructed their agency budgets, those salary allocations are used to calculate the fringe-benefit costs for next year's baseline budget. These costs include payroll taxes for Social Security and Medicare, paid to the federal government by the state in its role as employer, as well as pension contributions and health insurance. After slowing significantly in the mid-1990s, the costs of health insurance premiums were rising at double digits again as the new century began.

Baseline calculations are even more mechanical in many other areas. Rent budgets are adjusted upward by any contractually required rent increases. Utility payments are increased by appropriate inflation factors. The baseline budget for debt service is constructed by adding expected borrowing costs to existing payments for principal and interest. Again, the goal is to calculate the expected costs in the upcoming year for current levels of state services.

Before discussing areas where baseline calculations require more judgment we should stop to consider why the baseline concept, now used by the federal government and most states and localities, is so widespread. From a broad political perspective, the idea of current services mirrors the last adopted budget and therefore uses the prior year's legislative agreement as a starting point. From an agency manager's perspective the upward adjustments made in the baseline budget mean that the agency starts even in its budget battles without fighting for funds to pay for inflation or collective-bargaining adjustments, neither of which is under the agency manager's control. For the budget office the baseline *exercise*, as it is often called, forces some review of each major budget segment, if only to add in costs for annualization and to eliminate nonrecurring costs. The baseline also provides a starting point for budget making that is more or less consistent from program to program and agency to agency.

Finally, elected executives are attached to the baseline concept because it allows for a peculiar kind of budget miracle. Elected officials can adopt budgets that grow in actual dollars from year to year—and still take credit for sizable "budget cuts." The cuts, of course, are from the adjusted baseline. An example of this was the debate between President Clinton and House Speaker Newt Gingrich about whether to characterize savings in the Medicare program as "budget cuts" or "slower growth in spending."

The baseline concept is also criticized from time to time, and budget directors and elected executives experiment with changes aimed at responding to some of the weakness of baseline budgeting. For example, the baseline construct as described here creates no incentives for managers to improve agency productivity, because next year's baseline is based explicitly on current programs and staffing levels and implicitly on current management practices. So some budget offices trim down the baseline by a *productivity factor* of 1 or 2 percent and expect agency managers to maintain services through management improvements.

Governors sometimes seek to eliminate all legislative additions to the last budget, arguing that pork barrel spending is by its nature nonrecurring. Some legislative "adds" may pay for continuing programs, however, and governors and executive agencies sometimes find those programs appealing. Thus, any decision to remove all legislative additions from the baseline budget is likely to require many exceptions.

As a budget office constructs next year's baseline budget, the most difficult judgments are likely to involve workload-driven budget allocations and other areas where spending increases may not be controllable by state government. For example, a prison system may be expecting a higher inmate population, based on changing patterns of judicial action, including new sentencing laws, or on changes in parole policies. Should the baseline budget include those added costs, which may include new prison buildings and very large increases in head count for guards, or should budget making begin with the current population and staffing, to make it easier for policymakers to see the effects of new sentencing approaches?

The related question of mandates is equally difficult. Agency managers often argue that added spending is mandated by state or federal law, whereas budget officers believe that some discretion in spending levels may be possible. Governors and legislatures can change state laws, such as the sentencing rules cited above, and you can request waivers from federal mandates. Because mandates are frequently invoked to block spending reductions, you will do well to inquire into the basis of all so-called mandates and to request additional discussion and review of those you find objectionable on policy grounds. Beginning in the early 1990s the federal government has used administrative means to enlarge the scope of authority granted to the states in the design and operations of Medicaid, and Washington has legislatively devolved primary responsibility for welfare to the states. Although that devolution of federal programs and reduced regulatory oversight will, by definition, reduce the mandates associated with those programs and allow greater freedom for cuts in spending, those changes often come accompanied by reductions in federal funding, sometimes disguised as block grants.

Because the problems created by workload changes, mandates, and changing federal programs and funding do not fit easily into the baseline construct, you will often find them on your agenda during budget making, together with more straightforward questions about cuts from the baseline or increases to it.

A Note on Budget Systems

From time to time budget practitioners and chief executives become enamored of some new budget system. The most famous examples include the widespread adoption of Planning Programming Budgeting Systems (PPBS) in the 1960s, which required a multiyear analysis of different options for reaching programmatic objectives. Washington was also briefly infatuated with zero-based budgeting (ZBB) after Jimmy Carter became president. Carter argued that many programs funded within the current service baseline often received very little substantive scrutiny in budget making; he tried to use ZBB to review all programs every year. Good intentions notwithstanding, both of these systems soon bogged down under the weight of their own paperwork, and that experience has made budget professionals wary of new budget systems. The state of practice in governmental budgeting is far from ideal, however, and new initiatives to improve budgeting can be worthwhile. As you think through such proposals, you and your budget officer should ask yourself several questions:

- How will this new approach change the dynamics of budget preparation? Will it give us new ways to evaluate agency programs and spending or create incentives to improve management practice in the agencies?

- What kind of new data or materials are required to make this new system work? What are the costs, in time and effort, of collecting that data? How reliable will those data be?
- How will agency managers feel about this innovation? Will it seem rational and fair to them? Will one or another set of agencies receive advantage or be disadvantaged, or will it help to even the playing field for budget preparation?
- How will the legislature respond to this budgeting initiative? How might a new format or budget system change the dynamics of negotiations between the governor and legislative leaders?

New budgeting procedures, regardless of whether they are called new budget systems, can help the participants in the process ask new questions about state spending and see the budget from new and different perspectives. If agency heads can be persuaded to buy into the process, the results can be worth the additional work. But you should expect incremental improvement, not revolutionary change, and you should also expect some complaints and some negative effects as the innovations are put into effect.

Performance budgeting is the most important initiative in current budget practice. This effort, which focuses on refinements in cost accounting and the measurement of government services, has potential to improve management practice.[6] Performance budgeting is well advanced in a few states such as Texas, Florida, and Virginia. Oregon has also taken impressive steps to formulate long-term goals and benchmarks to measure progress toward those goals.[7] Performance budgeting is difficult to implement quickly, however, and requires several years of painstaking work. Measuring agency performance can be an important part of initiatives to improve service delivery. Published performance measures can also provide documented evidence of government's inevitable failures and mistakes, and those failures can be embarrassing to governors.

Baseline Spending on Capital Needs

The spending baseline may also include funding for a portion of the capital budget, where state government makes decisions about its long-lived assets, such as roads and bridges, prisons, other state buildings, and major equipment. It is difficult to apply the baseline concept consistently to this kind of spending. Some capital spending—highway maintenance, for example—looks very much like recurring program costs in the operating budget. In these areas the current services approach works well. Ideally, a government should establish a regular schedule for maintenance of all its capital facilities and include those costs, whether capital or operating, in the baseline budget. In the absence of an agreed-upon timetable for scheduled maintenance, budget examiners and agency personnel will typically bicker about what capital dollars, if any, fit into the current services conceptual framework, and building maintenance will be neglected in favor of more politically attractive programmatic needs. Eventually these deferred maintenance costs will find their way back into the budget in a more costly form as major rehabilitation projects for the state's buildings and other capital facilities.

Other capital projects—a new state office building, for example—are clearly one of a kind and do not fit into any imaginable current services baseline. Those projects often take several years to complete, however, and their continuing costs under existing contracts are an appropriate item for the spending baseline.

Is There a Gap or an Increment? The Preliminary Financial Plan

In these early stages of budget preparation the budget office is busy preparing revenue estimates and constructing the spending baseline. The goal of this important activity is a preliminary financial plan—a summary of projected revenues from existing sources and rates and the spending required to pay for current levels of services. Comparing these two totals allows the budget office to determine whether budget making begins with a deficit or surplus. As mentioned earlier, most states have experienced faster growth in spending than revenues, especially in arenas such as health care, corrections, and debt service. Therefore, this preliminary financial plan is likely to show a projected budget gap, even before proposals for new or expanded programs or tax cuts are added in. If your state is growing rapidly or the economy is at the peak growth period during the business cycle, you might be pleasantly surprised to find an increment instead of a gap. Before you spend those dollars on continuing spending programs or tax cuts, please look again at the discussion of cyclical surpluses in memo 2.

A *projected deficit* in next year's budget during budget preparation is very different from an *operating deficit* as the budget is executed during the current fiscal year. During budget making you will review options that allow you and the legislature to close a projected deficit by cutting spending or raising revenues. Although these choices may be unpleasant, you still have some time to resolve this problem before the new fiscal year begins. When an operating deficit arises during the current fiscal year, you will typically have less time, fewer options, and less cooperation from the legislature in closing any deficits.

You should stop and think before publicly announcing the size of a projected deficit based on early budget office estimates. General discussion about next year's tight budget may help set the tone for bad news in your upcoming budget, but the use of a specific number may prove troublesome. The projected deficit is likely to change in size as revenue estimates are revised, and announcement of a preliminary estimate may allow reporters and legislators to put you on the spot about the steps you will take to close that gap. If you decide that discussion of a projected gap has explanatory or tactical value, you should ask the budget office to prepare background material for you and your staff on the composition of the gap, as well as graphs or simple tables to help explain the problem to the press and public. The presentation of the executive budget is discussed in greater detail in memo 6.

Notes

1. See NASBO, *Budget Processes in the States* (2008), table 1, for information on votes required to pass the budget and table 10 for line-item veto authority.

2. In forty-six states the fiscal year begins on July 1. The exceptions are Alabama (October 1), Michigan (October 1), New York (April 1), and Texas (September 1).

3. Jeffrey L. McCaffery, "California: Changing Demographics and Executive Dominance," in Edward J. Clynch and Thomas P. Lauth, eds. *Governors, Legislatures, and Budgets: Diversity across the American States* (New York: Greenwood Press, 1991), 11.

4. In some states the economic and revenue forecasts are prepared by the revenue-collecting department, not the budget office. These estimates are neither more nor less likely to be accurate. In others forecasts are produced by a staff reporting to an independent panel or other consensus-forecasting mechanism. Again, consensus forecasts may reduce political squabbling over a governor's forecast, but there is little evidence that they are more accurate than budget office forecasts. Although the evidence on institutional consensus forecasting arrangements is weak, there is overwhelming evidence that combining multiple forecasts tends to produce more accurate forecasts. See Robert T. Clemen, "Combining Forecasts: A Review and Annotated Bibliography," *International Journal of Forecasting* 5 (1989); S. K. McNees, "Consensus Forecasts: Tyranny of the Majority," *New England Review* (November/December 1987): 15–21; William R. Voorhees, "More Is Better: Consensual Forecasting and State Revenue Forecast Error," *International Journal of Public Administration* 27, nos. 8 and 9 (2004): 651–71; Jeremy C. Weltman, "Using Consensus Forecasts in Business Planning," *The Journal of Business Forecasting* (Winter 1995–96); and V. Zarnowitz, "The Accuracy of Individual and Group Forecasts from Business Outlook Surveys," *Journal of Forecasting* 3, no. 1 (1984): 11–26.

5. Pew Center on the States and Rockefeller Institute of Government, *States' Revenue Estimating: Cracks in the Crystal Ball*, March 2011.

6. Performance budgeting has been an important topic of academic research and institutional analysis in recent years. For example, for discussions

of the growth of performance budgeting, its effects, and issues involved in implementing it effectively, see Yi Lu, "Performance Budgeting: The Perspective of State Agencies," *Public Budgeting & Finance* (Winter 2007); Yi Lu, Katherine Willoughby, and Sarah Arnett, "Performance Budgeting in the American States: What's Law Got to Do with It?" *State and Local Government Review* (August 2011); Kenneth A. Klase and Michael J. Dougherty, "The Impact of Performance Budgeting on State Budget Outcomes," *Journal of Public Budgeting, Accounting, & Financial Management* (Fall 2008); Government Performance Project, *Trade-Off Time: How Four States Continue to Deliver*, Pew Center on the States, February 2009; and US Government Accountability Office, *Performance Budgeting: States' Experiences Can Inform Federal Efforts*, GAO-05-215 (February 2005). For an earlier comprehensive review of performance management, including performance budgeting, see Dall W. Forsythe, *Quicker, Better, Cheaper: Managing Performance in American Government* (Albany, NY: The Rockefeller Institute Press, 2001).

7. See Jack Brizius, *Deciding for Investment: Getting Returns on Tax Dollars* (Washington, DC: Alliance for Redesigning Government, 1994). The Alliance for Redesigning Government is an affiliate of the National Academy of Public Administration.

Choices in the Final Phase of Budget Preparation

In the process outlined so far, you and your budget director have tried to work out a long-term plan consistent with your programmatic and political objectives. In reviewing preliminary revenue estimates you have also considered your tolerance for risk. In the hustle and bustle of taking office you may have also carved out some time to study descriptions of state programs and planned projects.

Now you will need to spend some larger chunks of time familiarizing yourself with the budget baseline and reviewing the choices that will go into your executive budget. The essence of budgeting is choice within constraint, and the toughest test of a budget office is its ability to describe those constraints and present the available choices on a timetable and in formats that make them useful to you.

Governor's Initiatives

With your programmatic priorities and campaign promises in mind, budget examiners, agency personnel, and your own staff have been working on detailed proposals to finance and implement those initiatives. You will also discover that your executive-branch agencies have proposals of their own that they hope you will embrace. Operating agencies will want to enrich existing programs or begin new ones. Your economic-development agency will argue for tax incentives and tax cuts. Your transportation department will present attractive proposals to expand road capacity and upgrade deficient bridges. The health commissioner may have ideas about improving medical care for children and poor people. In the absence of budget constraints you might like to move forward on all these initiatives. In the real world of limited budgets you will probably have difficulty finding funding for all your own priorities, much less those of the rest of the executive branch. Whatever the source, you need to come up with a list of specific proposals that will form the basis of your state-of-the-state address. Where funding is required these proposals must also be included in your executive budget.

Whereas your inaugural address might lay out your long-term goals and philosophy of government, the state-of-the-state address and the budget presentation are likely to be the two most detailed statements of your plans for the next year or two. One of the first managerial challenges for you and your top staff will be coordinating the content of the two documents. From the budget-making perspective this requires decisions on a timely schedule to ensure that funds are available to pay for your initiatives. Typically your programmatic staff will interpret your commitments broadly and seek to have initiatives included in the state-of-the-state address to help ensure their funding later. Your budget staff may take a narrower view and will seek to keep expensive programs out of the state-of-the-state speech except where your commitment is exceedingly clear. You or your chief of staff may have to referee.

From time to time the budget director will show you updated versions of the preliminary financial plan—the totals of spending and revenues that resulted from the baseline exercise and early revenue estimates. As discussion of your list of initiatives proceeds the costs of those proposals will be added to the spending totals (or subtracted from revenue estimates, in the case of tax cuts). If you were facing a projected deficit, it will now be larger. If you had an increment to spend, it will be shrinking.

With the budget office's support your agency heads will also present proposals designed to enhance computer systems or otherwise improve management practice. These *management initiatives* are not as politically attractive as many program initiatives, and you may find it difficult to choose among them. In tough budget years you will be tempted to turn down all such projects to reduce pressure on program budgets. If you fail to invest in management improvements, however, you cannot expect your agency heads to make speedy progress to change the way government works.

In a perfect world management initiatives and other proposals that claim to provide a return on investment would be evaluated and ranked with the help of cost-benefit analysis, discounted cash flow analysis, and other well-established tools of economic and financial analysis. Your staff will use these tools when practicable, and you should welcome and encourage this kind of analysis, even if you are not comfortable with all the technical details. Unfortunately, economic analysis requires lots of data and staff time, not to mention expertise, so you may not see these tools used very often.

Some state and local governments have successfully handled the selection process for proposed management initiatives by creating a competition for a limited pot of funding. Competing for a share of a statewide productivity fund can simplify and discipline the process of choice. After a bit of training your budget office and agencies can use the techniques outlined above to make these decisions the same way that business leaders plan their investments—on the basis of expected economic payoff. Under this kind of regimen the productivity investments you make now should make it a bit easier to balance the budget in the later years of your term. A disciplined plan for investment in productivity improvement will also provide evidence of your own managerial skills for those groups, such as business leaders, who worry about getting more services for their tax dollars.

If your state's credit rating is lower than you want it to be, you will want to consider another set of initiatives, which you might call your *fiscal agenda*. A careful reading of rating-agency reports on your state will give you a good sense of the problem areas as perceived by the credit raters. For example, your state may not budget according to generally accepted accounting principles (GAAP). If your budget includes receipts that are accelerated into the fiscal year or payments that are deferred, there will be a cost associated with a shift from statutory measures of budget balance to GAAP balance, like the costs of program initiative or tax cuts. For example, you may have to reduce any delays in paying your employees to get closer to GAAP balance, and taking that step may mean that you may have to raise more revenue or reduce programs to meet GAAP's more conservative definition of balance. Similarly, you may want to reduce the state's cash flow borrowing or speed up its contributions to its pension funds. If your state's debt load is a factor in poor ratings, you may want to reduce bond funding for capital during your term in office and pay for more capital projects on a pay-as-you-go basis, out of current tax revenues. Like productivity investments, these fiscal initiatives use up resources that you might prefer to spend on more politically attractive program initiatives; however, if your goal is an improvement in your bond rating, you are not likely to achieve that objective without disciplined adherence to a multiyear fiscal agenda.

In developing cost estimates for your initiatives you need to know the full annual cost of each proposal as well as the budget estimates for the upcoming year. First-year costs for a program or a tax cut may be modest if a program will be phased in or if a tax cut will be in effect for only part of the year. Full-year cost estimates, however, will help you understand the impact of these initiatives on the budget later in your term of office. Table 4.1 demonstrates one simple format that will help you keep the long term in mind as you consider this year's initiatives.

Table 4.1 Full-Year Impact of Budget Actions

Description of Initiative	First-Year Cost ($ millions)	Full Annual Cost ($ millions)
Job-training program—phased in during first fiscal year	4.3	8.0
Cut in corporate income tax—effective for last quarter of fiscal year	6.5	26.0

Gap-Closing Actions

So far we have been discussing choices that will add to the spending baseline or reduce the revenues projected in the preliminary financial plan. If you already are projecting a deficit, it will get larger when you add programmatic enhancements, tax cuts, productivity investments, and the costs of your fiscal-improvement agenda. If you began with an increment, you have probably moved to a deficit position. Now the choices become much tougher.

Spending Cuts

For some governors shrinking government is an ideological priority, and campaign promises may include a fairly detailed blueprint for budget cutting. For others cuts will be a pragmatic requirement to pay for new initiatives in other areas or to finance tax cuts. With low inflation restraining revenue growth and spending growing quickly in areas such as Medicaid, transportation, and education, projected deficits are the norm, not the exception, and governors usually try to balance the budget with spending cuts before raising taxes or fees.

On the other hand, when faced with spending cuts, most agency heads and program staff will advocate revenue increases. In making the case for new revenues they will point out that every dollar spent in every program has a constituency supporting it, inside and outside the agency. They may also point out instances where spending is needed to generate revenue. For example, cutting tax auditors may reduce tax revenue by amounts far larger than the savings from the personnel cuts. Agency and program staff may also argue that some spending is not "controllable" and cannot be reduced, because it is mandated by state or federal law or by court rulings. As suggested above, you should be skeptical about mandates and push to find out how those mandates might be changed. At the same time, you should recognize that a budget that does not balance without new federal actions or many changes in state law will be difficult to achieve and will cause concern during rating-agency review.

In theory, budgeting could be an exercise in rational economic analysis. The governor could look at the baseline budget, rank the state's programs from highest to lowest priority, establish an overall spending target that balances the budget, and then adjust spending in every program until the last dollar spent in each area brings the same amount of satisfaction. This rational approach would create a spending plan that most accurately reflects the governor's own programmatic and political priorities, but the result would be a significant redistribution of state spending. Redistribution of the benefits and burdens of government is likely to increase political conflict and make passage of the budget by the legislature more difficult.[1]

Alternatively, the governor could seek to maintain the political balance that resulted in the passage of the prior year's budget and respond to projected deficits simply by cutting from each program in the baseline budget by equal proportions. Across-the-board cuts can be defended as equitable, because every interest is treated equally. This approach may make legislative passage more likely, but it does not move a governor's programmatic agenda forward. Moreover, when substantial savings are needed, across-the-board cuts are likely to come up short. Many parts of the state budget are difficult to cut in the near term: Debt service is generally fixed; pension contributions cannot easily be avoided, although states have invented a variety of gimmicks to defer some of these costs; employee pay scales cannot easily be changed if the state is in the midst of multiyear contracts; some portions of the bureaucracy are funded by federal funds, and cuts do not generate savings for the state; and so on. Across-the-board reductions in the remaining areas—what we might call cuttable spending—may have to be very deep to generate significant savings.

In practice state budgets are simply too complex to allow the governor to allocate each dollar rationally, and few governors will sacrifice their own program priorities to across-the-board budget cuts. Therefore, a mixed approach is usually used. When cuts are required the budget office will begin with relatively painless cuts, as outlined below. If still deeper cuts are required, the budget office will protect a few programs from reductions, reflecting the governor's top priorities, and make approximately proportionate across-the-board cuts in the other program areas where spending can be controlled.

Some budget cuts can be almost painless. Recognizing that the starting point for budget cuts is the spending baseline, which has been increased for most agencies, your budget office will often begin with recommendations for cuts that should have relatively modest effects on agency programs and budgets. For example, instead of budgeting for full inflationary increases for supplies and materials, the budget office may propose trimming back the inflation factor. If this cut is proposed after several years of fully funded budgets, agency staffers are likely to agree that it will have little impact on programs. This is really just a mechanism for removing a cushion from an agency's budget and telling them to manage with a bit less money.

On the personnel side the budget office also trims dollars from the baseline for what is sometimes called *turnover*. Agencies are often unable to fill vacancies immediately, and incoming workers typically earn less than the workers they replace. Savings from attrition and lags in hiring, if not fully accounted for in estimates prepared by agencies, can be taken when the budget office reviews these requests. Again, agency staffers are likely to agree that some cuts against the baseline for this purpose are tolerable. Cuts in inflation adjustments and turnover are likely to be distributed by formula.

When the painless cuts have been made your budget office is likely to propose additional agency cuts, and this round of reductions may have significant programmatic effects. High on the list might be cuts in administrative staff. You may believe that agency overhead is too costly, but you will still have to count on those managers to run your agencies and implement new programs. Next may come cuts in service levels in low-priority programs that have few political supporters. Eventually you will also see recommendations for more serious cutbacks in more politically sensitive programs. Local aid might be cut back. These reductions might be packaged as block grants or accompanied by authority to raise local revenues, in hopes of providing political cover for the cutbacks. Medicaid recipients might be required to enroll in managed-care programs, which reduce costs but also reduce choice. Prisoners might be housed two to the cell instead of one, eliminating the need for capital spending for new facilities but increasing tensions in the prisons. Highway and bridge maintenance might be cut back, reducing the useful life of those facilities. Aid to state universities might be offset by higher tuition payments from students. As the cuts grow the programs you care most about will join the list of targets. At this stage your interest in revenue increases may revive.

Revenue Increases

If every dollar on the spending side has a constituency that supports it, every revenue increase has a constituency that will have to pay for it and will therefore oppose it. Economists generally argue for broad tax bases and low rates, to minimize how taxes affect the economic decisions of people and businesses. This is important to strive for but difficult to achieve politically.

Reasonable people can differ on the best political strategy for raising revenues. One school of thought argues that it makes sense to increase fees at least as quickly as inflation and to push up minor taxes before increasing the broader-based taxes, such as sales and income tax. Another set of strategists will argue that it is easier to get money from modest increases in the broad-based taxes and that the impacts on individuals will be less visible than annoying increases in many different fees and nuisance taxes. You can evaluate these two approaches yourself. You might also try to find out what view the legislative leadership in your state holds.

In considering revenue options your budget office will worry about several other factors. Staff will be concerned about tax increases that may make the state less attractive to businesses than its neighbors in the region. They will be concerned that additional sales taxes may encourage shoppers to travel to other nearby states to buy gasoline, retail goods, or cigarettes and alcohol. They will worry about the long-term growth potential of each new or expanding revenue source. For example, sales and income taxes usually grow over the longer term as fast as personal income in the state grows; cigarette tax revenue is likely to shrink over the long term. The budget office should also help you understand whether a revenue proposal is progressive—affecting upper-income groups more than less wealthy taxpayers— or regressive. For example, sales tax rate increases are likely to be regressive, because the poor spend a larger proportion of their income on taxable goods than do the wealthy. Your staff will also evaluate the impact of revenue options on different industries and on different regions of the state. Finally, they will care about the difficulties of implementing and administering new revenue options, a concern rarely shared by the legislature.

Issues such as revenue progressivity are frequently raised in the budget debate, but only occasionally are they elevated to the level of ideology. In 2003 Governor Bob Riley of Alabama presented a comprehensive proposal to increase taxes and make the state's revenue system more progressive. With support from several religious denominations the Republican governor and his supporters tried unsuccessfully to sell the package of tax increases and reforms as the kind of fair and moral action required by the New Testament. The proposal was defeated in a statewide referendum by a two-to-one margin, and the governor turned to spending cuts to balance his budget.

At regional and national meetings of governors you will learn of concerted efforts in a few areas to develop whole new sources of revenue. Over the years the National Governors Association has tried to get Congress to allow states to require mail-order and Internet vendors to collect sales taxes on catalog and online shopping. These taxes, although generally due, are rarely paid unless the seller is required to collect them. Officials in many states would also like to broaden the base of the sales tax to apply it to purchases of more kinds of services. When Florida and Massachusetts attempted on their own to tax a wide range of business services, however, the opposition was so vocal and effective that they quickly repealed those new levies.

From time to time governors also include large increases in federal aid in their budgets. For example, in 2010 Governor Arnold Schwarzenegger of California raised his estimate of federal aid in the 2010–11 budget from $3.4 billion to $5.3 billion in an effort to close particularly difficult budget negotiations.[2] The budget presented by New York's George Pataki in 1996 was balanced in part with $2 billion in anticipated federal actions. With the federal government trying to reduce its own deficits, significant new federal spending seems unlikely except in recessions or emergencies, so rating agencies and the financial community view such proposals with great skepticism. Many of the proposals to devolve federal programs to the states are structured as block grants with fewer mandates about how federal funds should be spent. Thus, decisions by the federal government to devolve authority to states may provide savings opportunities but only if the federal government is willing to maintain spending levels. This was the case with welfare reform at the end of the twentieth century. States can also save money on programs funded in part with federal revenues if they are willing to reduce spending and services to the recipients and providers of programs such as Medicaid. More often, however, federal block grants have been accompanied by decisions to cut projected spending in those program areas. In that case the states may find themselves looking for savings to handle those federal budget cuts at the same time they are trying to spend less from their own budgets on these programs.

Nonrecurring Actions

Just as you must be attentive to the long-term costs of new initiatives, you must also understand the multiyear impact of any gap-closing proposals. Once again, a simple way to pay attention to this question is to use a format like the one suggested in table 4.1 when reviewing gap-closing actions. Some gap-closers will save money in the upcoming year but not in the later years of your term. (Budgeteers sometimes call these the *out-years* of a multiyear plan.) Other proposals—such as borrowing for capital spending, issuance of bonds backed by payments from tobacco company settlements, or the sale of revenue-producing assets— may save money in the short run but add to gaps in years to come.

When pushed a budget office can often come up with sizable savings from nonrecurring actions. These gap-closers, however, come with a price. The credit-rating agencies and financial community track these actions carefully, and growing dependence on these *one-shots* is a significant negative in their evaluations of a state's credit.

In the normal course of events one-time savings opportunities will occur and so will nonrecurring spending needs. Rating agencies will tolerate the use of nonrecurring savings to fund one-time spending needs if the amounts are small and the trends stable.

You must understand that any nonrecurring action in next year's budget will have to be replaced—not in the indefinite future but in budget making just one year later. Dependence on one-timers will significantly increase the vulnerability of your budget during recessions. Budget oversight groups will attack with fervor what they will call gimmicks. In sum, then, one-timers are not the magical solutions they sometimes seem to be at the end of the budget-making process. In the world of state and local financial management the road to budget hell is paved with one-timers, not with good intentions.

Debt Financing

As suggested above, debt financing is another budgetary tool that can easily be overused in the final stages of budget making. A few states finance virtually the entire nonfederal share of their capital spending through the issuance of tax-exempt municipal bonds. A few other states, such as Nebraska and Wyoming, pay for virtually all their capital projects out of operating revenues or dedicated taxes. Most states fall somewhere in between, issuing bonds to finance some of their capital needs and funding the rest on a pay-as-you-go basis.

If your state relies on operating funds for some capital spending, program advocates will often suggest that you could free up resources for your initiatives and still move ahead on your capital program if you use bond financing instead. Your budget officer will remind you that the rating agencies will see a big increase in debt issuance as a negative factor in your credit picture. Temporarily increasing debt issuance and decreasing pay-as-you-go financing may make sense in a difficult economic environment. However, the same logic would suggest that you should cut debt issuance and increase tax-supported capital spending when the economy is strong. From time to time you may also encounter proposals to refinance some portion of your state debt.

Refinancings can in fact provide some budget relief, but those savings should typically be spread out over more than one year to avoid overreliance on one-time actions.

The arguments used by proponents and opponents of debt financing are both correct, of course, and investment bankers are always ready to help design a new bonding program. The problem with debt is that it has to be paid back, with interest, on an inflexible schedule. As bond issuance increases, so does the burden of debt service on your operating budget. As debt service increases, your ability to fund current programmatic needs decreases.

The wisest approach is to determine what level of debt issuance is consistent with the credit rating you want the state to attain and then budget for debt issuance at that level as a matter of policy. If that sounds too unimaginative you can follow the advice above and use a little less of that debt capacity during the growth years of the business cycle so you can borrow a bit more during recessions. Otherwise, you may find yourself with a nasty set of choices when the next recession arrives: deciding between (1) cutting back on your capital spending at exactly the wrong time in the economic cycle, (2) increasing your debt issuance and jeopardizing your rating, or (3) trying to find scarce operating funds to keep your capital program intact. In debt issuance, as in the rest of your budget, some reserve capacity will serve you well in hard times, so you should try not to use it all up to soften the painful but predictable crunches of annual budget making.

The Role of Agency Heads and Governor's Staff

During budget preparation your primary source of information and options will be the budget office. Many of those options will affect agency operations and programs, however, sometimes in significant ways. You may have already invited in one or more agency heads to work through particularly knotty issues with you and your budget staff. But you may want to make it possible for agency heads to make their case directly to you before you make your final budget decisions. The simplest approach is to set aside a block of time, as budget making draws to a close, for meetings with agency heads who feel the need for a final, personal appeal. These discussions should not be scheduled until final revenue estimates are available and you have made tentative choices about all outstanding issues. In the meetings you should be joined by your budget director and any other top staff who have participated in review of budget options. If the stories you hear from agency heads are consistent with the information you received in budget documents and earlier discussions, you can use the meeting to assure the agency managers that their concerns have been carefully considered and that their programs are being treated fairly. If you hear new information, you might ask a member of your staff to check further and report back to you later that day. You should not make any final decisions until you and your budget officer have compiled the full list of appeals and their costs.

Governors who prefer not to hear appeals directly can ask their chief of staff to make recommendations after meeting with agency heads. Other governors use programmatic specialists on their staff as a channel for agency concerns and to provide another source of information to test the recommendations of the budget office. As you listen to your agency heads and program staffers, you will be hearing arguments that preview the reaction of the constituencies served by those agencies. In theory budget staffers can also convey the expected reactions of interest groups to budget recommendations. In practice you may need more politically sophisticated advice to supplement information coming from the budget office.

Obviously, the reactions of these constituency groups will be an important factor in determining the legislature's reaction to your budget recommendations. Some interest groups carry special weight in statehouse politics. For instance, public employees who earn their livelihood on the state payroll care deeply about the decisions that are embodied in budgets, because those decisions affect their paychecks and their job security. If budget cuts and increases are important to public employees, the leaders of public-sector unions are also often important to elected officials. In many states union leaders are aggressive participants in elections, making campaign contributions to candidates for governor and the legislature and sometimes mounting grassroots campaigns, including television commercials, condemning budget cutbacks. Avoiding layoffs is typically the top priority of union leaders, and in recent years states and local governments have devised inventive methods to trim the payroll without firings, including early retirement and severance programs.

Legislators will also respond to programs and taxes that have a particular impact in their districts. At this final stage of budget making, as the budget office begins to put your recommendations into shape for publication, you and your policy and political staff must put this information about interest group and legislative preferences to use in formulating a plan to market your budget to the legislature, the press, and all the other groups who care about its contents. We will discuss this topic in more detail when we describe a typical budget presentation.

Notes

1. For a discussion of the politics of spending cuts see Robert D. Behn's classic article, "Cutback Budgeting," *Journal of Policy Analysis and Management* 4, no. 2 (1985): 155–77.

2. See Michael B. Marios, "California Budget Relies on More Federal Aid, Pension Rollback," *Bloomberg News,* October 6, 2010.

Budget Tactics: Laying the Groundwork for Adoption

Do you recall anything about the content of the first budget recommended by President Obama or the budgets proposed by President Clinton in his second term? If you are like most students of politics, all you will remember is that in most of those years the president's budget was DOA—dead on arrival—hours after it was presented. The point is simple: it is not the budget that you recommend that matters; it is the budget that gets adopted. It is not enough to present a carefully crafted, solidly balanced budget. You must get the legislature to adopt all or most of it if you want to make progress toward your strategic goals.

If you have served in a legislative office, you will have your own experience to supplement this brief discussion of the tactics of adoption. If you have not, your final budget-making sessions should include advisers with knowledge about your state legislature and its leaders.

By its nature legislative decision making is an untidy process. Using your own personal set of values, you can calculate and compare the benefits of spending an additional million dollars on tax relief, school aid, or social programs. Legislative leaders have to make those same calculations, taking into account the views of dozens or sometimes hundreds of colleagues. In most years the tactics you adopt before the budget is presented will have to be changed during actual negotiations, just as a football team usually alters its game plan as the actual contest proceeds. You will get more recent economic news as the adoption process continues. Interest groups and the press will not behave exactly as you predicted; neither will the legislative leadership. Nonetheless, it is important that you establish a tactical approach to guide the early stages of presentation and negotiations, if only to be sure that your own team begins with an agreed-upon series of plays.

The Economic and Political Setting for Budget Adoption

The legislative response to your budget will vary from year to year. As suggested above no one can predict with precision the factors that produce those variations, but four factors seem to affect budget dynamics on a regular basis: the economic setting; the extent of changes proposed by a governor or legislative leaders; the incentives for cooperation or competition among the leaders; and the political calendar.

In discussing these factors it might help to assume that legislators will apply a simple calculus in reviewing your budget proposals: They will want to take credit for spending increases and tax cuts, and they will want to avoid blame for budget cuts and tax increases. Oversimplified though it may seem, this basic calculus of credit and blame can be helpful in analyzing adoption tactics.[1]

The Economic Cycle

The dynamics of budget adoption at the low point of the economic cycle are very different from budget adoption during a period of peak growth. For reference consider your own choices under these two scenarios. During a recession you will be selecting from a list of painful alternatives—spending cuts, tax and fee increases, and ugly one-shots. When the economy is booming you will be able to cut taxes, increase spending, and still balance the budget, a cluster of outcomes that Mario Cuomo liked to call "a politician's paradise."

During a recession legislators will be seeking to avoid blame for all the pain in the recommended budget and to take credit for whatever steps they can take to mitigate those negatives. In short they will want to soften your spending cuts and reduce your revenue increases, if only by modest amounts. Typically they will have few scruples about the use of one-timers, because it will fall to you to repair any damage in the next executive budget.

During an upswing in the economic cycle the primary focus of the legislature will shift from avoiding blame to taking credit. Legislators will want to share credit with the governor for whatever good news was announced in the executive budget. They will also want to add enough to the spending increases or tax cuts to show that they are being responsive to the needs of their own districts or favored constituencies. As usual, they will see nonrecurring resources as an attractive tool for funding these needs.

When the economic situation is more uncertain legislative objectives may become more confused. As economic growth begins to slow, legislative leaders may find it more difficult to persuade their colleagues that the economic boom is over and that scarcity is the operative constraint. Similarly, after a long period of recession or very slow growth the first sign of economic pickup may stimulate a legislative frenzy to meet pent-up needs in their districts and among supporting groups.

The Scope of Redistribution

When elected officials try to bring about permanent and far-reaching changes in budgetary burdens and benefits, political conflict is likely to intensify, overwhelming the normal routines used by politicians to reach agreement. Redistribution creates winners whose share of the budget pie grows, as well as losers whose share declines or who pay a bigger portion of the taxes required to fund the budget. In some circumstances—when the budget pie is growing rapidly, for instance—the losers may not notice that their share is shrinking. When the economy is growing slowly and inflation is low, however, it is much more difficult to hide the losses suffered by one or another group in the budget arena. Inevitably those losers will look for politicians to blame. The result is often a group of elected officials who cannot organize themselves to follow normal paths to budget adoption.

Cooperation or Competition?

Another key factor in the tactics of budget adoption is the extent of cooperation or competition in your relationships with the leaders of the legislature.

Relationships may be competitive because of partisan differences or because of other factors. If both houses of the legislature are controlled by a party other than yours, the budget may become a weapon for partisan warfare, as it has been in Washington since the early 1980s. If your party controls both houses, the possibility of cooperation is greatly enhanced, although never guaranteed.[2]

As you might expect, the situation is even more complex when the legislature is itself split between two parties. You may be able to establish a strong-enough relationship with the leader from your own party to keep budget negotiations on track. In Albany, where control of the legislature has been split for decades, old budget hands used to opine that "two makes three," meaning that if any two of the three key leaders—the governor and the two majority leaders—could reach a firm agreement, the other leader would eventually have to capitulate. During Mario Cuomo's terms in office the two parties continued to divide control of the legislature, with the senate controlled by Republicans and the assembly by Democrats. The "two makes three" rule, however, seemed to operate effectively for only two years of Cuomo's last two terms in office, when an old friend from Cuomo's home borough of Queens became speaker of the assembly.

As this example suggests, other factors besides party allegiance can create a competitive relationship between a governor and a legislative leader. Deference to the chief executive is not necessarily a value that helps a leader win election in a legislature. Indeed, a newly elected legislative leader may find it necessary to do battle with a governor of the same party as a demonstration of independence. Alternatively a legislative leader may be thinking about a run for governor and may want to highlight disagreements with the governor's agenda. Finally, personal factors can also make cooperation difficult.

A governor with strong cooperative working relationships with both majority leaders has tactical options that are not available in other circumstances. It may even be possible to sit down with those leaders before the executive budget is presented and work out a script that will result in budget adoption on schedule, within agreed-upon financial parameters. A governor with a less cooperative relationship will be facing a much more fluid tactical situation.

In fiscally conservative Georgia, Republicans gained control in 2004 of the governorship as well as both houses of the legislature. This electoral coup followed a brief period of divided control and, before that, nearly a century of Democratic control. But undivided Republican control did not lead to political comity. Governor Sonny Perdue, who was barred from running for re-election in 2010, had to do budget battle with the two Republican leaders in the General Assembly. Both Lieutenant Governor Casey Cagle (who served as well in a dual role as senate president), and House Speaker Glenn Richardson were considered potential candidates for governor in 2010. Relations among these officials and between the legislature and executive were contentious. In the 2008 legislative session house leaders criticized the governor's revenue estimates and said he should get new economists. In 2009, as the effects of the financial crisis hit Georgia, Governor Perdue proposed eliminating the Homeowner Tax

Relief Grant (HTRG), a $428 million program of aid to local governments. The program was intended to enable localities to provide property tax relief to homeowners, but Governor Perdue argued that it was neither effective nor affordable. The legislative leaders labeled this spending cut a tax increase, leading to a stalemate that was not broken until federal stimulus money became available, allowing the legislature to fund the HTRG for another year. Without the political rivalries among these officials, budget debates might have been less acrimonious.[3]

Other factors shape the relationships between governors and legislative leaders. In some states informal rules of comity suggest that governors do not propose cuts in legislative budgets and that legislatures do not cut the governor's own staff. Violating these or other norms, including rules about when private discussions can be disclosed to the press, can damage otherwise cooperative relationships. If the legislative leaders do not volunteer information about any norms specific to your state, you might inquire in early getting-acquainted sessions with them.

The Political Calendar

The legislature will also approach budget adoption differently at different phases of the political calendar. As a rule the more time between adoption and their next election, the less sensitive will be the calculus of blame and credit. All else being equal, budget adoption will be more difficult in legislative election years and most difficult of all in the election year following reapportionment, when legislators will be running in districts with new boundaries.

You will feel some of the same pressures as the gubernatorial election year approaches. Thus, the best year to get difficult budget actions adopted is likely to be the year immediately after your own election, when you will be most willing to take the blame for tough budget-balancing steps and lawmakers will be less sensitive about their own election prospects. Governor James Florio of New Jersey, however, proved that even this time-tested tactic could go wrong. Elected in 1989 Florio moved quickly in the 1990 legislative session to raise sales and income taxes, expecting that these actions would give him financial breathing room when he ran for reelection in 1993. In 1991 the Republicans captured both houses of the state legislature. Moreover, New Jersey—like New England and the rest of the Northeast—was slow to recover from the recession. Still struggling to balance the budget in 1993 Florio was narrowly defeated by Christine Todd Whitman.

This simplistic approach to the political calendar can also mislead in a state such as California, where recalls are authorized. In 2003, only months after his reelection, Gray Davis found himself in a deep budget hole. The resulting stalemate in the budget process fueled a recall campaign, and the political incentives created by the recall effort in turn deepened and exacerbated the budget conflict. When Arnold Schwarzenegger, the newly elected governor, took office he was facing a staggering $38 billion projected budget gap over the next two years.

Legislators will also be concerned about the timing of local elections as they consider local aid allocations. In years when local officials are running legislators will be under more pressure to produce increases in aid—or at least avoid cutbacks—for their allies among local officeholders. In New York State the political calendar produces only one year in four—the year following a gubernatorial election—without races for legislative seats or any major local office.

Legislators and governors are not as sensitive to the federal election calendar unless the governor is a potential candidate for national office. In those circumstances legislative leaders of the opposite party have powerful incentives to use budgets or any other major legislative battlegrounds to embarrass a governor with an eye on Washington. Conversely, federal elections can sometimes create shock waves at the local level. The Republican victories in Congress in 1994 and 2002 shifted the balance in many state capitals and gave fresh hope to Republicans in states where odd-year elections are held. The shift was even more dramatic in 2010, when Republicans retook the majority in the House, gaining sixty-three seats—the largest midterm gain since 1938.[4] Republicans also won eleven governorships from Democrats, whereas Democrats won only five governorships from Republicans, giving Republicans a majority of governorships for the first time since before 2006.[5]

The Legislature and the Budget

Keeping in mind the twists and turns of the economy and the political setting for budget adoption, we can suggest some rules of thumb about the legislative response to executive budgets.

The legislature will not pass a budget including tax increases or significant spending cuts without leadership from you. To put the point more crudely, the legislature will need you to take the blame for tough gap-closing steps and will expect you to propose those actions.

The budget calendar allows you to get some credit for the good news, if any, in your presentation of the executive budget. The legislature is satisfied with this schedule because it also forces you to take the blame for the bad news. If you are not willing to provide cover for them, you cannot expect legislators to take tough budgetary steps on their own.[6]

One point worth remembering is that there is a small group of opinion makers who value fiscal stability and will give you credit for balancing your budget. Among them are the credit-rating agencies, the financial community, "good government" groups that focus on budget issues, some segments of the business community, and select newspaper editorial boards. If you need to improve the state's financial position, you will have to work hard to keep this budget-balancing coalition strongly in support of your fiscal agenda. Although these groups may not represent many votes, they can be important allies in otherwise lonely budget battles.

As a corollary to the first rule of thumb, you will find that *the legislature will not pass a budget that is more fiscally responsible than the one you give them.* Your budget will provide a guidepost for budget balance and important clues about the level of gimmickry you are willing to tolerate. But the legislature will want to mitigate whatever pain you have caused to their favored constituencies and will have a list of programs and projects they want for their districts. Solving these problems will take additional resources. It is the task of legislative staff to find those resources in a way that causes as little additional political pain as possible. Often, this will mean stretching the boundaries of budget balance with changes in revenue estimates, one-timers, or even more flagrant gimmicks. Alternatively, they may find those resources by cutting back your own initiatives, especially those without broad constituencies. Obvious targets will be items on your fiscal and productivity agendas.

In California in 2011 Jerry Brown, returning to the governorship after twenty-eight years, proposed a budget nearly devoid of gimmicks, counting in part on the assumption that legislators would allow citizens to vote on a proposition to extend expiring taxes. But this stance did not survive the legislative process: A small minority of legislators blocked the vote. The legislature adopted a budget the governor found unacceptable, he vetoed it, and the budget as finally adopted relied, among other things, on a $4 billion upward revision to revenue estimates.

If your executive budget is solidly balanced and itself eschews gimmicks, you can take a stronger stand for fiscal responsibility with the legislative leaders. If you can persuade the majority leader of one or both houses to sign on as a partner with your fiscal agenda, you may get some help in keeping legislative damage to a minimum. But the leaders will have to find resources to respond to the needs of some members, especially those in closely contested marginal districts.

This suggests a final rule of thumb: *To keep the budget process from deadlocking, you and your budget officer will have to help the legislature leaders solve its problems.* If you want the legislature to fund your initiatives and avoid gimmicks, you may have to be ready to help lawmakers find less distasteful sources of funding for their needs. This point will be raised below, in the discussion of the negotiating process.

These generalizations are labeled rules of thumb because they are useful, but imperfect, guides to practice. In 2003 the legislative leaders in New York raised taxes to reduce budget cuts proposed by the governor. Instead of giving cover, the governor lambasted lawmakers for "job-killing tax increases" and vetoed their budget changes. The legislature overrode the governor's vetoes. After fiscal crises legislators will sometimes advocate more conservative budget practices than the governor, and in a few states in the south and elsewhere the governor and legislature will vie to produce more conservatively balanced budgets. In view of the variety of circumstances and political cultures in statehouses around the country, it is not realistic to articulate iron laws of budgeting for state governments instead of rules of thumb.

The Elected Finance Officer—A Wild Card in Budget Negotiations

If your state elects an independent finance officer, you need tactics that take this additional player into account. On the one hand, the elected treasurer or comptroller (to pick the most common of several titles) typically plays little or no role in budget negotiations, except in an agency head's role as claimant. On the other hand, the elected finance officer often plays some role in presenting the state's credit to the financial markets, so this official's views on the budget can have impact.

If your goal is to keep the finance officer as your ally in the budget battle, you should take some or all of the following steps:

- *Consultation on the fiscal agenda:* For an elected finance officer, the fiscal agenda is the primary substantive arena. He or she may have legislative proposals or suggestions for improving the state's procurement procedures, debt practices, or accounting practices. You should keep those proposals in mind as you prepare your own fiscal agenda, sharing credit with the finance officer from time to time.

- *Adequate funding for the finance officer's budget:* As you look for budget cuts to balance your budget, you might ask your budget officer, who will typically be the liaison to the finance officer, to keep a careful eye on the adequacy of funding for that office. The finance officer's help as an ally may be more important than the modest savings you can achieve through harsh budget cuts.

- *Early briefings on budget issues:* The elected finance officer needs to look smart about the state's finances but is usually positioned outside the mainstream of budget communications or negotiations. He or she needs timely information from your budget officer to avoid looking uninformed or ill prepared.

Management of the state's finances involves a wide range of activities, beginning with budgeting but moving on to more mundane and less visible areas, such as debt management, financial reporting, internal control, and debt collection, to name a few. Because these issues have little political or policymaking significance, you will rarely be called upon for decisions in these areas. If your state has an elected finance officer, your executive-branch appointees to budget and finance positions will have to work in concert with the elected official's staff to get these routine but important tasks completed. This partnership at the technicians' level must continue to work, even during those periods when you and the finance officer are feuding.

Notes

1. See Behn, "Cutback Budgeting," on the credit/blame calculus.
2. Only Nebraska's governors have the luxury of a unicameral legislature.

3. See Thomas P. Lauth, "Budget Deficits in the States: Georgia," *Public Budgeting & Finance*, Spring 2010.

4. See http://elections.nytimes.com/2010/results/house.

5. See http://elections.nytimes.com/2010/results/governor.

6. For a helpful discussion of these dynamics in Washington, see Joseph White, "Presidential Power and the Budget," in Thomas D. Lynch, ed., *Federal Budget and Financial Management Reform* (New York: Quorum Books, 1991), 1–29.

Going Public with the Budget

The presentation of the budget concludes the largely private work of preparing the executive budget and kicks off the adoption phase of the process. You will have at least two obvious objectives during this brief but intense period of activity: first, to show that you have some mastery of the budget and its content; and second, to select several themes that you want the press to highlight so that they stand out from the scores of initiatives and issues dealt with in the budget. Less obviously, you want to start off on the right foot with the legislature as the adoption process begins.

Your Script for the Unveiling

Working from your strategic plan, you began the budget-making process worrying about a few issues and themes of special concern to you. But many other problems have bubbled to the surface during your review of budget options. As you complete your decisions, you and your staff need to look up from the detail and refocus on key themes so your speechwriters can begin to prepare the script for your budget presentation. Indeed, those themes should already be apparent in the budget message, which prefaces the printed volume of the budget and serves to introduce it, and these two statements of policy should be prepared simultaneously—or at least frequently cross-checked—until the budget goes off to the printer.

While your speechwriters work on your text, your budget and public-information staffs will be producing graphics to accompany your presentation. Modern computer software and projection equipment allow speedy preparation of high-quality graphics, and you should use them to good effect in your presentation. Similarly, the text for your presentation, like most of your important speeches, should be reprinted as needed for distribution to the press. Your public relations officer will determine the deadline when all but minor editing must cease.

Unlike many of your other speeches, your budget presentation is likely to be full of numbers and facts. The schedule for completing the script must include time for all those details to be checked for accuracy by budget staffers. It is embarrassing to find a budget total in the printed budget different from the one in your presentation. The production schedule for your presentation should also include time for one or more full rehearsals, with speech text and graphics. Because of all the numbers and budget jargon, budget speeches are different from most of your presentations. Similarly, graphics can be awkward to handle. A rehearsal provides a useful opportunity for practice and critique.

Early Press Leaks

The budget office will be working hard to keep budget details confidential until their public unveiling in your presentation. On the other hand, the press will be probing for early information. It is probably sensible for your press officer to feed them a few details that you want made public in the days just before the presentation rather than let them grill agency heads and lobbyists who may prefer to provide them with negative stories. One approach is to preview the central themes in the presentation by releasing illustrative program details. For example, if children's issues are going to be a focus of your presentation, your staff might leak information about increases in a specific program for children.

A very different approach is to use early leaks to emphasize themes that might not get noticed after the budget has been released. For example, in Massachusetts, Governor William Weld's budgets were fiscally conservative, emphasizing tough budget management and such themes as privatization. Just before budget presentation, however, Weld and his staff leaked details of increased allocations for some social service programs, presumably to counterbalance the more conservative emphasis of the budget itself. Governors have used this tactic for bad news, too. In 2011, on the day before his budget was scheduled to be released, Michigan Governor Rick Snyder leaked to the Associated Press his plan to make hundreds of millions of dollars in cuts to state universities and local governments, coupled with targeted aid for universities that kept tuition increases below 7 percent and additional funds for local governments that share services. This leak emphasized Snyder's theme of rewarding institutions that constrain spending.[1]

Finally, governors and their staffs have used leaks to divert attention away from their actual plans and confuse their opposition. As Governor Lowell Weicker was preparing a proposal to enact Connecticut's first income tax, one Hartford reporter came into possession of a faked document that described in some detail a fictitious plan to balance the budget with a sales tax increase. This diversion gave Weicker and his staff a few extra days to prepare before the opponents of the income tax marshaled their forces. Needless to say, this last tactic is risky and can alienate the press.

Internal Briefing Materials

While your speechwriters and public information staff are preparing your script, you and your staff should also be reviewing briefing materials prepared for your private use. The objectives of these materials are, first, to help you master some of the many details contained in the budget and, second, to be sure that you, your staff, and your agency heads are all giving the same answers to the most important questions you will be asked.

For this reason you may find it helpful to receive most of this material in question-and-answer format. You, your staff, and the budget director might begin by listing the most difficult questions you think you will be asked. Budget examiners, program staff, and agency heads may all be pulled into the process of writing up answers. The more pointed the questions, the more useful the process. By the time you go public with the budget, you and your staff should have a common understanding of how you will answer most of the questions you are likely to be asked.

As you prepare for your presentation you may feel as if you are back in college, poring over binders of briefing materials, underlining and outlining, and reviewing answers to anticipated questions. This work is necessary and useful, but you should avoid becoming overly consumed by program or budget detail. As governor, your main job is to emphasize the key themes in your presentation and show that you understand the broad issues and key facts in the budget. You do *not* have to memorize every number in the budget. When your questioners ask about minor details, your budget officer can respond, or you can ask them to hold those questions for a separate briefing session with budget staff after your own presentation is complete.

The Press Release and Related Materials

In addition to preparing your speech text and graphics, the public information office will be preparing a summary press release on your budget. This document will typically provide more detail than your speech, but less than the governor's message in the printed volume. Again, the press release should hammer away at your key themes. A press release that tries to list all relevant details will, by definition, fail because of its lack of emphasis. The budget is the detailed document; the press release must be focused and thematic.

You might also find it useful to release short issue papers on important initiatives or other special topics, including new or expanded programs, proposals for changes in aid formulae, or your fiscal and management agendas. If you are certain that the press will want a specific set of budget facts—year-to-year growth comparisons, for instance—you might include them in the briefing packet. Most of these issue papers will be based on the briefing materials you have been reviewing and will require little extra work to produce.

Printing, Production, and Other Technical Details

While you are getting ready for your public presentation, the budget staff is getting final numbers and text prepared for publication in the printed budget volumes. Your final decisions will be loaded into the budget office's database and incorporated into the budget message, program descriptions, and other supporting material. Budget schedules, graphics, and text will be checked for errors and prepared for printing.

Although the printed budget volumes and their online versions are the reference documents most visible to the public, the executive budget will also be introduced in the form of legislation, so budget examiners will be preparing specific appropriation language reflecting your decisions. Similarly, budget staff, together with your counsel's office and agency staff, will be preparing any other legislation required to implement the budget. New tax bills may be required, as well as bills changing statutory aid formulas or abolishing or initiating key programs. In some cases, particularly with tax bills, you and your staff will need to flesh out important details of your policies that were not addressed in the public budget documents. You may need to make decisions about unexpected issues that arise in this period. Failure to meet statutory deadlines for the submission of these materials may give the legislature an excuse to delay its own adoption schedule.

While this production and drafting process is under way, the budget officer will also be preparing more technical briefing materials for another important audience—the credit-rating agencies. Unless yours is one of the few states that are not active in the debt markets, analysts at the rating agencies will be expecting to sit down with your budget staff shortly after your presentation to review the executive budget in detail. As indicated earlier they will be looking for structural budget balance, a budget free of gimmickry, and progress toward a clearly defined fiscal agenda. They will also be concerned about the legislative reaction to your budget. A governor's budget that the legislature will likely reject is no comfort to the rating agencies.

Credit ratings reflect the agencies' judgments about your state's ability and willingness to repay its debt on a timely basis. They are based on budget performance, economic and demographic trends, and debt loads, and on the capabilities of the management team running the state's finances. If your budget officer is not known to them, the raters will want to take his or her measure and assess the strengths and weaknesses of the managers and top technicians in the budget office. From time to time they will want to meet you as well. In discussions with you they will not be expecting to meet a hands-on financial manager. Rather, they will be trying to evaluate your commitment to maintaining or improving the state's financial position and practices and your ability to get legislative agreement with your fiscal agenda. Although they may not expect to find the same sense of fiscal responsibility in the legislature as they find in you, they do care about legislative attitudes and particularly about your ability to work with the legislature. Legislative dysfunction was one of the reasons Standard & Poor's gave when it downgraded US long-term debt from AAA to AA+ in August 2011. As the S&P report put it, "The downgrade reflects our view that the effectiveness, stability, and predictability of American policymaking and political institutions have weakened at a time of ongoing fiscal and economic challenges."[2]

Early Briefings

You and your staff will want to organize briefing sessions for several special audiences shortly before the budget is released. These may include your own agency heads, legislative leaders and their staff, other key elected officials, and the leaders of a few especially influential interest groups. During or after some of these meetings, you or your staff might point out that positive comments to the press will be appreciated. An interest group leader or elected finance officer might be prompted to praise those parts of your program in their issue area if your budget includes initiatives in their program or policy arena.

Agency heads: You or your chief of staff should conduct a briefing session for the heads of your operating agencies. As budget preparation concluded, they should have been informed about recommendations for their own agencies, so your briefing should focus on two broader topics. First, you should remind them of the broad themes you will emphasize when the budget is presented. Second, they should be reminded of your expectation that agency heads will support the governor's budget in public and private, even—or especially—if they do not agree with the choices you have made in their agency budgets. Working with the clients and providers involved with their programs, your agency heads can help sell your budget, or they can work to undermine it. You should make it clear that loyalty is an important value in your administration and that you expect active and energetic support for all your budget proposals from your own appointees.

Legislative leaders and staff: As you prepare to make the budget public, try to give some early information to the legislative leaders and staffers in whose hands your fate now rests. Several channels can be useful for these communications, including calls from you to the leaders, briefing of their staff by yours, and early delivery of the budget documents to legislative staff, perhaps the night before public release. The timing and level of detail of these briefings will reflect norms and practices in your own state. The obvious goal is to get the adoption process launched without unnecessarily annoying your legislative counterparts.

At this point the legislative minorities deserve special mention. In most circumstances the minority leaders and members of each house will play little meaningful role in budget negotiations. Their votes, however, can be important when the majority's margin in one house is very small, when a supermajority is required to pass the budget (as in Arkansas or Rhode Island), or when you are marshaling votes to block an override of a veto. Thus, you may find that it is a good tactic, as well as good manners, to provide such courtesies as early briefings to the minority leaders, especially when they are members of your own party.

Other elected officials: As suggested above, an early briefing can help maintain a positive relationship with an elected finance officer. He or she will want to review the fiscal and management initiatives included in the budget and learn enough about the budget to avoid being caught off guard by reporters' questions.

You or your staff could also call big-city mayors or other important local officials to outline your local-aid provisions, changes in mandates, or other key recommendations affecting their communities.

Interest group leaders: Finally, the heads of interest groups that have supported you, or others who are affected positively by your budget, should receive phone calls informing them of the proposals that are most important to them. Again, the goal will be to brief them before they are called by reporters and to ask them to make supportive comments in response to press inquiries. Some of these calls can be delegated to your agency heads and program staff. Others might be made by your chief of staff or budget director. You will be the best judge of which leaders should get personal calls from you.

Show Time

After the hours you have spent in budget making, reviewing briefing materials, and rewriting and fine-tuning your speech and press materials, you will be well prepared for budget presentation. You will certainly know much more about this set of recommendations than anyone who will be questioning you, and your budget officer and staff are available to respond to detailed queries.

In New York governors usually began their presentation, often called budget school, with a performance of the speech and slide show before the statehouse press. (New York legislators did not seem to be distressed to receive their briefing later in the day. In other states briefing the press before the legislature might constitute a major breach of protocol.) Mario Cuomo, always masterful in public question-and-answer sessions, spent more time responding to questions than he did on his formal presentation, which typically lasted about three-quarters of an hour. Cuomo seemed to enjoy even partisan and argumentative questions from Republican backbenchers. A governor with less enthusiasm for that kind of give-and-take might choose to spend a larger share of the scheduled time on the formal presentation and less on questions.

Cuomo also invited the editors of the state's newspapers to the governor's mansion for a third presentation and dinner that same evening. In states where the capital is in the largest city, the governor, the press officer, and the budget director might instead visit editorial boards after the formal presentation is complete.

Failure to court the press and reach out to the public can harm your agenda. Governor Rick Scott of Florida, who won election by a narrow margin, took office in January 2011 facing a very difficult first budget and planning significant cuts in state spending. Press and public support was crucial. But his early press relations were abysmal. Most newspapers in the state had endorsed his opponent, and during the campaign his press officer reportedly said, "Rick Scott gets better use of his time going straight to the voters than trying to convince misguided editorial board members to endorse him."[3] During his first few months in office he did not meet with editorial boards and reportedly avoided reporters and news shows.[4] His disapproval rating in Quinnipiac polls rose from 22 percent in February of 2011 to 57 percent in May before improving slightly in August. Only 24 percent of respondents knew that the budget he signed did not include any tax increases.[5] According to one Republican strategist, "His team has done a very poor job of selling. . . . It doesn't have to do with policy so much as personnel. They came in and they had a very adversarial relationship with a very aggressive Florida press corps. The salesmanship of a difficult product has to be done with a little bit more finesse, instead of with stonewalling."[6] Recognizing the damage this was causing, the governor began a charm offensive to reach out more aggressively to the press and the public, with uncertain results as this memo was being written.[7]

All this work should pay off in the press coverage of the budget. Careful preparation of press briefing materials will help get your themes good play in the news stories, and briefing of the editorial boards will usually produce some helpful commentary over the next few days. Courting the press is hard work, but it is easier than repairing damaged relationships.

Talking to the Voters Directly

As communications technology improves, governors are making much more elaborate efforts to speak directly to the voters, cutting out traditional intermediaries such as interest group leaders and the mass media. Posting budget documents on state websites has become routine, but governors often devise more innovative strategies.

When budget shortfalls jeopardized budget balance in the commonwealth of Virginia, Governor Douglas Wilder used homey metaphors and simple graphics in statewide satellite broadcasts to explain to voters the forces creating growth on the expenditure side. Virginia also published a tabloid newspaper on the state budget. This *USA Today*–style publication was distributed in libraries, and the text and graphics were made available to community newspapers. Wilder also convened summits with business leaders to review budget issues. The governor's staff concluded that this educational effort made it easier for the legislature to trim back popular programs, including their own legislative initiatives.

In Oregon Governor Barbara Roberts initiated what she called her "conversation with Oregon" in 1992, using town meetings and closed-circuit teleconferences to discuss with voters the budget options available to respond to ballot initiatives limiting property taxes. Roberts did make cutbacks in the state workforce and other spending reductions but could not get voter acceptance for a tax increase to help close the projected budget gap. In Connecticut new governor Dannel Malloy went on a listening tour, visiting seventeen venues around the state after releasing his 2011–12 budget.[8] After the end of the tour he proposed shifting some of his proposed tax increases from the middle class to wealthier citizens.[9] In California Pete Wilson's budget office was an early adopter of new technology, creating a simple computer simulation of the fiscal year 1996 budget and posting this budget game on the Internet. The simulation was designed to explain the governor's budget choices and convince players that Wilson's choices were preferable to other alternatives, such as tax increases or deeper spending cuts in key areas. These simulations have become quite popular, with variants existing in Maine, Massachusetts, Minnesota, New Hampshire, Ohio, Texas, and Utah.[10] Many are sponsored by outside organizations and are not designed to guide users to support the governor's choices but rather to illustrate the difficulty of those choices.

Governors, budget offices, legislators, advocacy groups, and the press now regularly use new media such as Facebook,

Twitter, YouTube, and RSS feeds to communicate directly with voters about budgets and budget policy choices. You will want your staff to be on top of these evolving technologies and to incorporate them into your overall media strategy.

Interest group leaders have also adopted new methods of reaching out beyond their own membership to voters at large. In several states budget battles have occasioned televised and print ad campaigns from public-sector unions, antitax groups, and other organizations. In response, state party organizations or legislative campaign committees have also created political commercials tailored to budget battles. To date, these initiatives seem limited to budget disputes that propose significant tax cuts or increases or that propose sharp service cutbacks or layoffs of state workers.

New York has had a long history of powerful interest groups taking to the airwaves to oppose cuts or reforms in Medicaid and other large programs. This marketing had been very effective at stymying gubernatorial efforts at reform. During the 2011–12 state budget debate supporters of Governor Andrew Cuomo struck back with similar tactics. The Committee to Save New York, supported by the real estate industry, bankers, and business executives, ran television advertisements opposing tax increases, supporting Medicaid reform, and supporting the governor's agenda in other ways.[11] Governor Andrew Cuomo had an extraordinarily successful first budget, achieving much of his agenda.

Notes

1. Zane McMillin, "Snyder Set to Propose Deep Cuts to Universities, Cities," TheStateNews.com, February 17, 2011, www.statenews.com/index .php/article/2011/02/report_snyder_to_propose_deep_cuts_to_universi ties_cities.

2. Standard & Poor's, *Research Update: United States of America Long-Term Rating Lowered to 'AA+' on Political Risks and Rising Debt Burden; Outlook Negative,* August 5, 2011.

3. Tristram Korten, "The Right-Wing Roots of Scott's Press Strategy," The Florida Independent, http://floridaindependent.com/11719/the-right -wing-roots-of-rick-scotts-press-strategy, October 28, 2010.

4. See Patrick Crowley, "Florida Gov. Rick Scott's Marketing Crisis," www.crowleypoliticalreport.com/2011/04/florida-gov-rick-scotts-market ing-crisis.html, April 6, 2011; and Rachel Weiner, "Rick Scott: The Most Unpopular Politician in Florida?" www.washingtonpost.com/blogs/the -fix/post/rick-scott-the-most-unpopular-politician-in-florida/2011/05/25/ AGv5aQBH_blog.html.

5. Quinnipiac University, "Florida Gov's Approval Goes from Terrible to Bad, Quinnipiac University Poll Finds," August 5, 2011. www.quinni piac.edu/x1297.xml?ReleaseID=1633

6. See Rachel Weiner, "Rick Scott: The most unpopular politician in Florida?"www.washingtonpost.com/blogs/the-fix/post/rick-scott-the-most -unpopular-politician-in-florida/2011/05/25/AGv5aQBH_blog.html.

7. Elise Hu, "Florida Gov. Rick Scott's Tanking Polls Lead to Charm Offensive," August 6, 2011, www.npr.org/blogs/itsallpolitics/2011/08/05/ 139029361/florida-governors-tanking-poll-numbers-leads-to-charm -offensive, and David Royce, "His Poll Numbers Diving, Rick Scott Seeks Help from Snubbed Estate: The Press," FlaglerLive.com, August 1, 2011, http://flaglerlive.com/26065/rick-scott-media.

8. Mark Pazniokas, "Malloy Closes Budget Road Show on a Humble Note," *The CT Mirror*, April 12, 2011, www.ctmirror.org/story/12211/ malloy-closes-raucous-night-humble-note.

9. Mark Pazniokas, "Malloy Proposes Easing Tax Increase on the Middle Class," *The CT Mirror*, April 14, 2011, obtained at www.ctmir ror.com/story/12236/malloy-proposes-trimming-his-middle-class-tax -increase-300.pdf.

10. See Christopher Conte, "Honey, I Shrunk The Deficit! Computer Games Offer Citizens the Chance to See How Government Works and the Trade-Offs Involved in Policy Making," *Governing*, December 2003, www .governing.com/topics/technology/Honey-I-Shrunk-The-Deficit.html.

11. Charles V. Bagli, "Business Group Prepares Plans to Counter Unions," *New York Times*, January 7, 2011. www.nytimes.com/2011/01/08/ nyregion/08save.html.

The Legislative Phase of the Budget Process

With budget presentation complete, you may experience some sense of frustration. You have worked hard to craft a budget that reflects your goals. You have tried to give it every political and public-relations advantage as you introduced it to the world. Now you have to step back and leave it in the hands of the legislature. Eventually lawmakers will tell you how they want to reshape it. Your staff can help you guess about the schedule that the legislature will follow, using recent history as a guide. Although you can continue to sell the virtues of your budget choices in forums around the state, as a practical matter you can do little to speed up the legislative process. Indeed, legislative leaders often need deadlines such as the end of a session and a new fiscal year to get their members to act. In that case trying to accelerate the process of budget review and negotiation may simply give the legislature time to make more changes in your budget without speeding up final passage. In short, prepare to wait.

Early Responses

For a day or two after all the hoopla of budget presentation, the media will carry reaction stories from interest groups, legislators, and local leaders. Like most of the news these stories will generally be negative, covering the complaints of those who feel short-changed by the budget.

A period of relative quiet will follow, occasionally interrupted by the release of a legislative staff analysis designed to explain the budget to the members or to find ammunition to take shots at you and your recommendations. When you ask your legislative liaison to check on the reaction to the budget among the members, you may hear about a few sore points, but the general message is likely to be, "They haven't really focused on the budget yet—it's too early in the session."

Interest groups will convene their members to complain about their treatment in the budget and lobby for more spending or deeper tax cuts. You or your spokespeople will respond, reiterating the rationale of your selection and the virtues of the budget as a whole. Legislative hearings will feature your agency heads, who will repeat the administration's line, while legislators sympathetic to their programs try to cajole them into asking for higher levels of funding. And you will wait some more.

Two-Way Negotiations

You may be anxious to join the final battle on the budget, but the next operational step must be negotiations between the legislative leaders, who will be trying to come up with a mutually agreeable list of changes to your budget. In some states, such as Massachusetts, those two-way negotiations do not begin in earnest until the public release of complete budget proposals by each house. In other states the process may take place behind the scenes. If a very narrow majority holds control of one house, a small number of members can hold the margin of votes required to enact a budget. As a result it may take longer to come up with an agreed-upon position in that caucus, slowing the process of two-way discussions. Small minorities of legislators can also play a disproportionate role in states that require a supermajority to pass the budget. In 2010 voters repealed California's long-standing requirement that the legislature pass a budget by a two-thirds majority in each house. Arkansas and Rhode Island are the two remaining states that require a supermajority for virtually all appropriations.[1]

For the most part the preferences of each majority caucus will change little from year to year, and veterans of the budget wars will be able to predict where and by how much the budget is likely to change. The legislature is also likely to need funds for district-specific projects, grants, or programs, similar to the pork barrel projects (or earmarks) added by members of Congress to the president's budget. In Maryland the legislature amended the 2011–12 state capital projects budget to add $15 million to fund individual projects, $7.5 million for each house, including items such as an ecology learning center for the Boy Scouts and a boiler room for the Little Sisters of the Poor.[2] These allocations, called member items in New York, turkeys in Florida, and walking-around money or simply WAMs in Pennsylvania, are likely to be your least favorite additions to the budget. For many individual legislators, however, these items are the top priority in the budget and, as such, can be an important tool in the leaders' effort to put together a majority to pass the budget.

While the leaders are sounding out members and beginning to discuss a joint package, legislative staff will be searching for resources to pay for the needs in that package. With more recent information about the economy and tax collections, they may argue that revenue estimates can be increased. As the fiscal year draws to a close, underspending in some parts of the current budget may lead them to argue that those sections of agency or program budgets can be cut painlessly. If you did not cut your spending baseline to balance your budget, they will do so now, looking for so-called easy cuts such as inflationary increases to budgets for supplies and materials or turnover savings. In legislative parlance this sometimes is known as *denying inflation*, a label that irritates agency heads who have to live with the undeniable reality of rising prices. In the first stages of their search for resources to pay for members' needs, legislative staff and leaders will try to avoid politically painful steps, such as tax increases, program cuts, or layoffs.

Eventually the two majority leaders will come up with some joint proposals. Because their goals, very broadly defined, are to avoid blame and take credit, their list will typically include spending to add to favorite programs or to offset cuts you proposed, and tax cuts—or at least smaller tax increases than you recommended. Their list, however, may also include elimination of some of your key initiatives. The leaders may have strong political or policy differences with some of those initiatives, but they may also be targeting your pet proposals for negotiating purposes. As bargaining proceeds you will be offered the opportunity to buy back some of your initiatives by coming up with your own alternative sources of funding to pay for legislative needs.

The Governor Rejoins the Process

While you are waiting for the leaders to conclude their two-way negotiations, you might think again about your goals in the adoption process. If your budget was a solidly balanced and politically well-conceived first step toward your strategic objectives, your most desirable adoption scenario would be passage without any changes. Legislators typically make only marginal changes to a proposed budget, and it is theoretically possible that in some very difficult economic circumstances the leaders would decide that their best course of action would be to pass the budget unchanged and blame the pain on the governor. It is much more likely, however, that they will seek to "improve" whatever budget they receive.

The second most desirable adoption scenario might be a carefully scripted process in which legislative changes are minor and do no real damage to the government's financial position. During Ed Koch's first term as mayor of New York City, which began in 1978, he and his staff successfully stage-managed the passage of several budgets, underfunding a few legislative priorities, such as the budget for cultural institutions and the public schools, and helping identify appropriate sources of funds to restore those needs. He had two unusual advantages in this process. First, the city's budget was still under close scrutiny from the Emergency Financial Control Board, and that oversight helped sustain a vivid memory of the city's recent fiscal crisis. Second, deference to the mayor was a central norm of personal conduct for the incumbent majority leader of the city council. Governors typically have much stronger legislatures to deal with.

Even in these advantageous circumstances Koch's ability to choreograph the adoption process began to break down before his first term was over. As legislators push the boundaries of the budget process, they may learn that they can in fact make more changes to the budget without causing immediate damage to government or suffering significant retaliation. If so, it would be rational for them to keep pushing. Moreover, elected representatives at the state level are more likely to believe in legislative activism than in deference to the executive, as demonstrated by the growth of legislative staff.

Elected chief executives learn, too, and some of them lose patience with conservative budget tactics. In New York City Koch may have wondered why the local legislature got all the credit for spending on school programs. As the memory of the fiscal crisis dimmed and the city's economy thrived, he may also have wondered why the budget could not be stretched to accommodate additional spending without higher taxes. By the time Koch ran for a fourth term in 1989, it was becoming increasingly evident that the city's budget was structurally unbalanced. His successors in office are still battling to keep the city's budget balanced.

In short, it is not likely that you will be able to control completely the outcome of the adoption process. Legislative leaders are likely to give you more latitude in the first year of your first term, but they will also be under pressure from their members to achieve more than in past negotiations. In some states with fiscally conservative political cultures, those appetites will be constrained by long-standing norms supporting fiscal stability and high credit ratings. In other states no such constraints exist, and legislators of both parties will support tax cuts even at the cost of fiscal stability. In general, as you look ahead to the conclusion of bargaining, you cannot expect the legislature to care as much as you about structural budget balance or to keep its requests for changes within the programmatic and financial limits you propose. To achieve the most sensible budget possible, you may have to help find the resources to meet some of legislators' needs and use your veto to eliminate other additions to the budget.

Three-Way Negotiations—Concluding the Bargaining Process

If regular meetings between the governor and the legislative leaders are a practice in your state, you and those leaders may decide to meet from time to time even before they have arrived at a joint position, and these meetings may be helpful in conveying some sense of activity and movement, if not necessarily progress. Staff-level meetings can also be useful in explaining your budget proposals and getting preliminary indications of legislative reaction. Real bargaining cannot fruitfully begin, however, until you receive a complete list of the changes to your budget proposed by the leaders, including their suggestions for funding the needs they have identified.

Without a clear sense of the financial impact of the legislative package, you cannot decide how to respond. In states with a nonpartisan legislative budget office, your budget director may accept the estimates produced by those analysts. In other states legislative staffers may come up with much more optimistic numbers than your own budget office did. In any event, until your budget staff reviews a detailed listing of the leaders' proposed changes, you will be unable to assess their financial impact.

Like the other documents you used in budget making, you need to see an analysis of the full annual costs of the legislature's package, as well as the impact on the budget now being negotiated, so you can understand how the recommended changes would affect your strategic budget plan.

Timing is an important element in budget negotiations. If you unveil proposals that provide additional resources before receipt of the legislative list, the leaders are likely to increase their demands. If you hold back information about new financing sources until they present their package, you can propose that those resources be used to buy back initiatives being held hostage by the legislature or to eliminate the most risky of their funding proposals.

Similarly, you may have soured on some of your own proposed cuts or revenue measures after seeing the political reaction to them. This presents a negotiating problem of some delicacy. On the one hand, the legislature may have already agreed to respond to those complaints themselves, in hopes of getting credit with the affected constituencies. On the other hand, you may want credit for those repairs yourself. From a financial perspective your wisest course of action is not to backtrack on any of your own budget recommendations until you have seen a completed version of the legislature's changes. If lawmakers decide to eliminate those troublesome proposals, they might also intend to finance those changes. If you ask for changes in your own budget, you can be sure that the legislature will ask you to pay for them and increase its own needs accordingly. In 2003, in the midst of negotiations with the city council, New York's Mayor Mike Bloomberg announced the restoration of some of his own proposed cuts after passage of the state budget provided additional resources. The predictable result was delay in the final stages of budget adoption and an increase in the council's demands.

In sum, then, you should hold off for as long as possible making your own proposals for changes in the budget you presented. Ideally you should not act until you have received and reviewed a complete list of joint legislative proposals for budget amendments. If you move before the legislative leaders do, they will have a powerful incentive to delay, in the expectation that you will take further steps that will be helpful to them.

A final note on timing: During bargaining, the leaders will ask for your agreement not to veto their new spending proposals. You should reserve your right to veto legislative additions until you have seen the appropriation language passed by the legislature. New items may be added at the last minute, sometimes without discussion with the executive and without offsetting cuts or revenues. Neither can you be sure until final passage that the legislature has enacted all agreed-upon revenue proposals. The veto may be your only available tool to balance the adopted budget.

Big Personalities, Strong Feelings, and the Role of Staff

When actual bargaining begins, the participants may be able to proceed rationally and calmly—and quickly—to a conclusion. Governors and legislative leaders, however, are likely to be strong personalities, and budgets are typically the most important legislative actions in a session. Mirroring the dynamics of budget negotiations in Washington, the battle over the budget can easily become a skirmish in a broader partisan battle between political factions, political parties, or political rivals. Even without such additional baggage, governors can find bargaining sessions with their legislative counterparts unpleasant and frustrating. The leaders and their fiscal staffs usually have had many years of experience in budget negotiations, and they may be skillful at pushing to the limits in those bargaining sessions. For example, they may lowball estimates of the costs of their proposed additions to the budget. For this reason you must be careful not to accept cost estimates put forward in a negotiating session between leaders without review by your own staff. Your budget office may have significant disagreements with the legislature on the cost of spending items or the value of savings or revenue proposals.

Often you will face pressure to strike an incomplete bargain. Enacting a budget requires resolution of many issues, some of them complex, and it is tempting to put some aside for later consideration. The mechanisms for delay can vary. Budgets sometimes include spending, savings, or revenue increases that are contingent on policies that will be detailed by legislative action later in the year—policies that are agreed pursuant to a chapter of law. In New York Governor Andrew Cuomo's first enacted budget included a variant on this idea, with expenditure savings in Medicaid that were contingent on as-yet-unidentified actions to be taken by a committee of stakeholders in the health care industry. Although the pressures to assume savings or revenue contingent on unknown future actions can be great, postponing action on key budget questions can freeze operational planning and also add risk to the budget—risk that, if large enough, can cause consternation among the rating agencies.

With so much at stake it is not surprising that big personalities might give vent to strong feelings in the course of negotiations. In some cases a blowup can clear the air or even move negotiations forward. Warren Anderson, who served for many years as majority leader of the New York Senate, used to storm out of budget negotiations every year. For Anderson, who retired in 1988, the walkout signaled the start of the final round of horse trading, not a breakdown in talks.

It is also possible for strong feelings to hinder negotiations and harden bargaining positions. For this reason governors and legislative leaders often delegate much of the day-to-day haggling to staff and use face-to-face meetings between the principals for other purposes, such as breaking deadlocks or announcing agreements.

The Legislature Votes

Eventually the legislature will vote on a budget. Most of the time that vote will take place before the next fiscal year begins or within a very few days thereafter. Legislative leaders may also use delay as a tactic, however, postponing passage while the new fiscal year begins, in hopes of achieving larger gains.

The likelihood of significant delay increases if members of the legislature perceive that they will suffer few costs using that tactic. One kind of cost is disruption in government. When workers and vendors do not get paid and local governments do not receive expected aid payments, the political cost of delay is obvious. When the US Congress fails to pass appropriation bills on time, the device of the continuing resolution is often used to maintain the flow of checks to workers and vendors, so the cost of delay can be modest. States like New Jersey, where the use of emergency appropriations is legally restricted, suffer fewer delays than do states like New York and California, where the use of emergency spending bills has become routine. If the governor's assent is required for the passage of emergency bills, you can raise the cost of legislative delay by withholding your approval. On occasion, if disputes are severe enough, the budget can be delayed even after the state shuts down parts of government. In Minnesota in 2011, after the July 1 deadline passed, Governor Mark Dayton shut down highway rest stops, closed state parks, suspended the lottery, and stopped issuing liquor licenses and cigarette tax stamps. After more than two weeks (a long delay by Minnesota standards) and much public frustration, the governor and legislature reached an agreement on the budget.

In some states constitutional limits on the length of legislative sessions make budget delay much more difficult. Even without those limits budget delays may create another cost for legislators by disrupting their schedules. In states where the fiscal year begins on July 1, a stalemate over the budget keeps the legislature in session into their recess, when vacations and campaign dates have been scheduled. In New York the fiscal year ends on March 31, but the legislature typically remains in session until the end of June, so legislators suffer no scheduling problems if the budget is not passed on time.

Legislative leaders without the negotiating leverage to make substantive changes in the budget may resort to delaying tactics to prove to the rank-and-file legislators that the leadership has made extraordinary efforts to meet members' needs. If positive goals such as tax cuts or spending increases cannot be achieved, leaders can show the governor up as an ineffective leader by delaying passage of the budget.

Even if legislators plan to pass a timely budget, they are still likely to wait until the last possible moment. Deadlines help the leaders force decisions from their members about their needs and priorities. Once leaders agree, legislative technicians still have to redraft the appropriation and tax bills to incorporate any changes. In a flurry of action, often late at night, those bills will be passed and sent on to you.

The Governor's Veto

As suggested earlier, the budget appropriation bills passed by the legislature may contain unexpected language changes or new spending items. Indeed, the legislative leaders may have included some new items expecting that you would use your line-item veto.[3] When the budget is passed the budget office reviews the bills in detail to be sure that the adopted budget is fiscally sound and to point out any programmatic problems that may arise from changes in appropriation language. When that review is completed, staff will make veto recommendations to you. Your political advisers will point out that the items singled out for veto have supportive constituencies that will be upset when the veto is exercised. Your budget officer is likely to respond that regular but measured use of your veto will strengthen your hand with the legislature and may cite Franklin D. Roosevelt, who used to ask his staff to "bring me something to veto."

In considering vetoes, governors must also be concerned about avoiding overrides. If a successful veto adds weight to a governor's influence with the legislature, an override can badly undercut that influence and can lead legislators to believe that they can oppose a governor with impunity. As suggested earlier, some attention to the needs of minority leaders can help avoid that unwelcome outcome.

The governor's veto can be used selectively to conclude the legislative process and help ensure a balanced budget. When a governor is confident, however, that an override will not succeed, a veto can be used more boldly and may help cement gubernatorial power. In 2011 Governor Chris Christie in New Jersey vetoed $1.3 billion of spending in the legislature's adopted budget. Despite controlling both houses of the legislature, the Democratic majority could not muster the two-thirds vote needed to override even one of the thirty-nine vetoes they considered.[4] A veto can also lead to political breakthroughs. In Florida in 1983 Governor Bob Graham set out to increase taxes to raise teachers' salaries and fund other education initiatives. After much wrangling, the legislature passed a continuation budget that did not raise revenues for education. Graham vetoed the legislature's entire school aid budget, together with a few pork barrel items critical to the legislative leaders. Graham followed up the veto with a quick barnstorming trip around the state, and the legislative leaders agreed to pass a more generous school aid budget, funded by new corporate taxes, higher alcohol taxes, and a mandated increase in local school taxes.[5]

Once in a while a governor may find that legislative overrides of gubernatorial vetoes produce a positive result. In 2003 Governor George Pataki swore that he would not agree to a budget funded by what he called "job-killing" taxes and proposed a package of extensive cuts to balance the executive budget. The legislature, divided between Republican and Democratic control of the two houses, agreed to a package of tax increases that eliminated most of the cuts and provided additional resources to help New York City balance its budget. Pataki vetoed the tax increases but did not campaign hard to get individual legislators to vote against the overrides, which ultimately were successful. The mayor of New York praised the resulting budget, and most interest groups were satisfied with the result. Some political observers speculated that, after months of declining polls, Pataki might have also found the outcome acceptable. Old Albany hands, however, worried that the legislature would learn to like making budgets without the governor's acquiescence and that the governor's influence on the budget process would diminish.

Notes

1. See National Conference of State Legislatures, *Supermajority Vote Requirements to Pass the Budget: A Legisbrief* 6, no. 48 (November/December 1998, updated October 2008).

2. See http://mlis.state.md.us/2011RS/budget_docs/2011_bb_funding .pdf.

3. In all but six states governors have some form of line-item veto, according to NASBO, *Budget Processes in the States* (2008), table 10.

4. Richard Perez-Pena, "New Jersey Governor Vetoes Spending," *New York Times*, June 30, 2011.

5. See Paul Starobin, *Governor Bob Graham and the Improvement of Florida's Education System* (Cambridge, MA: Kennedy School of Government Case Program, 1984).

MEMO 8

Budget Execution

When a balanced budget has been adopted and you have approved it, your direct involvement with budgetary issues will usually cease for several months. In the budget office and the agencies, however, much more work remains to be done as the fiscal year begins. Agencies are typically asked to prepare a detailed *spending plan* putting into effect the broad programmatic guidelines and new totals in the adopted budget. On the basis of these plans the budget office releases some or all of those allocations to the agency, and the business of government proceeds.

You may find yourself drawn back into the budgetary arena for several reasons. If your budget officer believes that the adopted budget is not solidly balanced, the budget office may recommend holding back the release of agency funds in a managerial effort to cut spending. Agency heads and legislators may protest, arguing that this caution is unwarranted or that this unilateral action is a breach of your agreement with the legislature.

You may think about breaching that agreement yourself if you find some legislative initiatives particularly repugnant; however, you are likely to be back at the same table, negotiating with the same legislative leaders, when your next budget is presented. Unless the budget is badly out of balance or some serious political or policy issue is involved, it makes sense to treat the adopted budget as an implicit contract between you and the legislature and to encourage your agency heads and budget office to work hard to maintain both the letter and the spirit of that agreement in its implementation. Unilateral decisions by chief executives not to spend as the legislature intended have been potent sources of conflict between the two branches. If Watergate had not pushed Richard Nixon out of the White House, his second term might have been remembered for a different constitutional crisis—a battle between the president and Congress over budget impoundment. Similar struggles have taken place in a number of states.

You may also find budgetary issues back on your agenda if major deficits or surpluses arise as the fiscal year progresses. The budget office compares planned spending and revenues with actual levels and analyzes discrepancies. This *variance reporting,* as it is usually called, is designed to provide timely warning of inaccuracies in budget estimates. Often budget modifications, sometimes called *supplemental* or *deficiency budgets,* must be presented to the legislature to realign appropriations. If variances are not dramatic, this may be primarily a technical bill to fine-tune agency appropriations. If the budget is badly out of balance, you may have to recommend more dramatic steps, such as additional spending cuts.

Midyear budget gaps present grave challenges for governors. In some states governors are limited in their ability to adjust spending after budget adoption. In New York, for example, the courts have determined that the executive has no authority to adjust school aid, Medicaid, and aid to local governments during the year. These program areas constitute the bulk of state spending. New York governors can withhold appropriations for state agencies, but spending on state operations represents only about 26 percent of nonfederal spending.[1] A 10 percent cut in 26 percent of the budget effective for the last six months of the fiscal year would generate savings of about 1.3 percent; however, tax revenue can fall 5 or even 10 percent short of projections when the economy turns down suddenly. Governors in many other states have much greater ability to cut the budget during the fiscal year but still face legal and practical limits when they act on their own.

Governors can do more with the assistance of the legislature—midyear tax increases are rare but not impossible, as are sizable cuts in spending areas over which the governor does not have unfettered control. But the incentives for cooperation from the legislature are not compelling. Why should they share the blame with a governor for midyear spending cuts or tax increases when in a few short months the governor will detail a more complete program for budget balancing in a new executive budget?

Public progress reports on the operating budget will be required several times during the year. Your budget officer will probably have to visit the credit-rating agencies again shortly after budget adoption to review the financial plan for the new fiscal year. Indeed, rating agencies sometimes upgrade or downgrade a state's credit rating on the basis of the adopted budget. The state will also have to produce a public update on its finances when it markets notes or bonds, and other public reports may be required by statute. For example, some states produce public updates every three months, like the quarterly reports of large corporations. As noted above, the SEC requires speedy public announcements of material financial events, in an effort to give investors timely information about changes in the state's credit quality.

A Note on Courts and Budgets

Decisions by state and federal courts can impinge on the implementation of state budgets, sometimes dramatically. In New York the top state court overturned a decision by the governor and legislature to change the actuarial methodology used by the state employees' pension fund and ordered the state to repay nearly $3 billion to the pension system. Serious disruption of the state's finances was avoided when the pension system agreed to phase in the additional contributions over seventeen years.

Some state courts across the country have overturned school-financing formulas and made decisions with important budgetary impact in other areas, such as Medicaid cost containment. In the 2010–11 New Jersey state budget, Governor Chris Christie and the legislature cut education spending significantly, a move challenged by advocates for students in low-wealth urban districts. In May 2011 the New Jersey Supreme Court ruled that the cuts denied these students their constitutional right to a "thorough and efficient education" and required the state to fully fund its 2008 School Funding Reform Act, a decision that increased state spending by $500 million.[2]

Federal courts have also been important players in several budgetary arenas, requiring additional state spending to upgrade client care in institutions housing the developmentally disabled or to reduce prison overcrowding, for example. In 2011 the US Supreme Court ruled that overcrowding in California prisons, which housed double the number of prisoners they were designed for, constituted cruel and unusual punishment and that "without a reduction in overcrowding, there will be no efficacious remedy for the unconstitutional care of the sick and mentally ill in California's prisons."[3] The decision is expected to lead to the release over several years of tens of thousands of prisoners and gave impetus to Governor Jerry Brown's plan to move more inmates to county jails.[4]

Unfavorable court decisions tend to come in clusters after recessions and other periods of budgetary stress, as state officials and legislators push the limits of the law in their efforts to maintain or regain budget balance.

State courts are also claimants on their own in the budget arena. As large and costly operating agencies, court systems look for additional state funding to pay higher salaries, maintain systems of courthouses, and keep up with what is often a growing caseload. As a separate branch of state government, the judiciary is sometimes advantaged as a budgetary claimant by special constitutional protections. In New York, for example, the budget for the courts must be included in the executive budget as the chief judge submits it, although the legislature is free to increase or reduce it.

It would be impossible to prove that state court decisions are influenced by the judiciary's success or failure as claimants in the fight for resources. It is noteworthy, however, that the New York pension decision and several other costly court decisions on budget issues followed a very public battle between Governor Mario Cuomo and New York's chief judge over the budget for the court system, a battle that the governor won, perhaps at great expense. The savings extracted from the courts in that fight were dwarfed by the costs of overturned budget actions.

Notes

1. See Robert B. Ward, *Gubernatorial Powers to Address Budget Gaps during the Fiscal Year*, The Nelson A. Rockefeller Institute of Government, June 17, 2010.

2. See *Abbott v. Burke* (M-1293-09), May 2011, available at www.edlaw center.org/cases/abbott-v-burke/abbott-decisions.html.

3. See *Brown v. Plata*, available at http://lawprofessors.typepad.com/files/09-1233-1.pdf.

4. See Jennifer Medina, "Prison Ruling Raises Stakes in California Fiscal Crisis," *New York Times*, May 23, 2011.

A Final Word on Strategy and Tactics

As your term progresses you will fill the empty spaces in this broad overview with your own experience about the unique practices, terminology, and vocabulary of budget making in your state. Although this book may still be useful to you as a checklist, its value as a primer will disappear as your familiarity with state budgets grows. In that welter of detail, however, you should never lose sight of your two critical roles—as strategist and tactician—in the budgetary process and the importance of the budget in achieving your broader policy and management goals.

Your long-term policy and political goals are the substance of the budget strategy that should inform the choices you and your staff make in each budget. It will be your words and actions that keep your appointees focused on those central goals. Another central strategic goal should be fiscal stability, which allows you to progress toward your more substantive goals without the disruption caused by budget deficits. Although nothing can completely shield your policy and political initiatives from the vicissitudes of the business cycle, a structurally balanced budget will provide you with some protection in recessions. Thoughtful preparation, including but not limited to reserves accumulated during the growth period of the economic cycle, can provide additional insurance against the politician's worst budget nightmare—a recession in an election year.[1]

As the most visible figure in the budget arena, you are also the cornerstone of each year's negotiating tactics. A lot rides on your success in the budgetary arena. Obviously your political and substantive objectives will suffer if you are not victorious in these budget battles. So will your state's financial position, because a strong executive influence is generally critical to the maintenance of structural budget balance. Your objective is clear—to get each budget adopted in a form that advances your longer-term strategy. Although those long-term goals might not shift much from year to year, your adoption tactics must change to reflect the economic climate and political calendar and to keep the legislative appetite for additional spending and tax cuts under control. Every year, you and your staff must work out a detailed plan of tactics to get each budget enacted, the way a coach of a football team works out a new plan for each game. And development of that plan for adoption must begin during budget making, because tactical concerns will shape your decisions about spending and revenues. Unlike the football coach, however, you will be the most important player on your budget team, as well as a major contributor to the development of the tactical plan.

Some tactical thrusts will succeed. Others will backfire as the economy changes or the legislature responds in unexpected ways. Nonetheless, by beginning the adoption process with a clearly articulated plan of action, you are more likely to get a budget that meets your strategic and financial goals than by settling for improvised tactics.

If you cannot use the budget to state your goals and move state government in the direction you advocate, you are not likely to make much progress toward those goals. As your term ends, voters and the press will find it difficult to say what you have accomplished. If you have mastered the budget and adoption process, you will have a solid list of tangible achievements. Effective use of the budget as a policy and political tool is a necessary, if not quite sufficient, condition of successful leadership in the statehouse. Do everything you can as soon as you can to grab hold of the budget process and make it work for you.

Note

1. Budget professionals and the rating agencies are still struggling to refine and elaborate approaches to managing budgets through the budget

cycle. For years the credit rating agencies argued that states should achieve specified target levels of rainy-day funding, but those levels were rules of thumb—5 or 10 percent of tax revenues, for example—and were not related to shortfalls suffered during recent downturns. More recently the rating agencies have been asking states to run recession scenarios in their economic projections to estimate how much protection different levels of reserves might provide. Adequate reserves and scenario planning are growing in importance because state tax revenue has become more volatile in recent decades, as evidenced by record-setting revenue shortfalls in the last two recessions. (See Richard Mattoon and Leslie McGranahan, "Revenue Bubbles and Structural Deficits: What's a State to Do?" Federal Reserve Bank of Chicago Working Paper 2008-15, November 1, 2008; and Pew Center on the States and Rockefeller Institute of Government, *States' Revenue Estimating: Cracks in the Crystal Ball,* March 2011, for discussion of these issues.)

The rating agencies have also argued that nonrecurring actions should be avoided during the boom segment of the business cycle, implying that unavoidable one-shots encountered during upturns—refinancing savings, for instance—should be added to reserves. A few states have adopted policies aimed at increasing pay-as-you-go financing for capital when the economy turns up, with the expectation that debt financing would increase during downturns. Governors and their budget officers sometimes invest portions of a cyclical surplus in productivity initiatives, aimed at producing recurring savings in the future. In much the same way cyclical surpluses can be used to reduce debt. In 2010 Massachusetts adopted a novel approach to reducing the impact of revenue volatility, limiting to $1 billion the amount of capital gains revenues Massachusetts can use in its operating budget. Revenue above that amount must be deposited to the state's rainy-day fund. The Fitch rating agency said that "this change is a budgeting policy improvement as it will reduce the volatility of the Commonwealth's budget."

All these tactics can help a state to prepare for economic hard times. But, as this is being written in 2011, the budget paradigm is only slowly evolving to take into account the vicissitudes of the economic cycle, and the budget literature provides little in the way of explicit guidance about how governors and budget directors should prepare for the next recession.

Appendix: Budget Vocabulary

Newcomers to budgeting can be put off by the jargon peculiar to the craft. The terminology used in state and local budgeting is different from the federal jargon, and some states and local governments use terms that are unknown elsewhere. But as states and local governments move to generally accepted accounting principles (GAAP) for financial reporting and, more slowly, for budgeting, the technical vocabulary for budgeting is becoming more standardized. A number of budget offices try to make their documents more accessible by including guides to financial terminology, and those seeking to make sense of the budget of a single jurisdiction should check to see whether the document includes a glossary.[1]

Budgets and the Budgetary Process

When presented, a budget is an estimate of revenues for the next planning period and a proposal for spending those revenues. This proposed budget is typically called the *executive budget* or the *governor's budget*. The date of the presentation of this budget proposal is usually specified by statute or in a state's constitution.

After review of the governor's budget proposal, the legislature modifies it and enacts its own version. In most states a governor can also use the *line-item veto* to cancel some of the changes made by the legislature, and the legislature in turn can attempt to *override* those vetoes. The budget that survives at the end of this process is usually called the *adopted budget*. In a budget process that is functioning as designed, all these actions are completed before the beginning of the *fiscal year*, which is the basic accounting period used by the state. Nearly half of the states adopt *biennial budgets,* spanning two fiscal years. In all but four of the states, the fiscal year begins July 1 and ends June 30. After the initial adoption of the budget additional changes may be made by the legislature to a budget as it is executed. These modifications are sometimes called *supplemental* or *deficiency appropriations.* The executive branch is usually authorized to make more modest changes in the allocation of funds without legislative action.

The executive budget proposal includes information in three formats: a *financial plan,* which is a comprehensive outline of the main elements of the revenue and spending proposals; the more lengthy books of tables and text describing the specific elements of the budget proposal; and *appropriation bills* presenting the budget for adoption by the legislature. The appropriations bills are usually accompanied by other *budget bills* that make changes in permanent statutes authorizing spending programs or revenues to bring them into conformance with the governor's proposed budget.

As outlined below budgets and financial reports use a number of technical terms to describe spending according to different accounting definitions. Legislatures, however, use *appropriations* as their spending unit. An appropriation is a statutory authorization to spend, not a planned or actual amount of spending, and under some circumstances a state may spend much less than the appropriated amount. For example, the legislature may appropriate the full cost of a planned capital project in one fiscal year, but actual spending may take place over several years. In those circumstances the unspent amount may be authorized again year after year as a *reappropriation.* Less frequently the executive branch may choose not to spend money appropriated by the legislature because of policy disagreement or fiscal conditions. A governor's legal authority to withhold spending varies from state to state, and no standard terminology exists. Drawing on the federal vocabulary, executive-branch actions to block spending might be termed *impoundments, rescissions,* or *sequestration,* depending on the statutory structure and the rationale for with-holding appropriated spending.

Governmental Accounting

As suggested earlier, states and local governments typically pre-pare *financial statements* after the budget has been executed and the fiscal year ends, as required by GAAP. The rules of GAAP are promulgated by a body called the Governmental Accounting Standards Board (GASB).[2] One important element of GAAP is the requirement that state and local governments report on spending in several key funds on a *modified accrual basis*, which differs in important ways from the *cash basis* of accounting used by the federal government and preferred by legislatures and ear-lier generations of financial managers. GAAP requires financial statements to go beyond reporting of the cash disbursed and re-ceived during its fiscal year in a format analogous to a check-book. GAAP also requires financial managers to estimate taxes owed to the state but not yet paid and expenses incurred by the state and not yet paid. These adjustments made to the *receipts* and *disbursements* used in cash-basis accounting are called *accru-als*. For example, if the state has ordered and received equipment but not yet sent out a check in payment, an expenditure accrual would be included in the financial reports. After these adjust-ments required by GAAP the terms used to describe financial inflows and outlays are *revenues* and *expenditures*, as summarized in table A.1. *Full accrual accounting*, the model used in the private sector, is used for some government units that are expected to be self-supporting and is also required for government-wide report-ing, as outlined in GASB's Statement 34, promulgated in 1999. Under full accrual accounting a state is required to report *depre-ciation* on capital assets as an expense or use a surrogate measure for depreciation.

When revenues exceed expenditures in a given budget period, an *operating surplus* is produced. These surpluses increase the *fund balance* on the state's *balance sheet*, which reports its *assets*

Table A.1   Basic Accounting Terminology

Basis of Accounting	Revenue Terminology	Spending Terminology
Cash	Receipts	Disbursements
Modified accrual	Revenues	Expenditures
Full accrual	Revenues	Expenses

and *liabilities*. Alternatively, when expenditures exceed revenues, an *operating deficit* results. Over a period of years annual operating deficits can produce a *fund deficit* or *accumulated deficit* on the balance sheet.

GAAP also requires state and local governments to report their financial results in a complex *governmental fund structure.* Most spending and taxes are accounted for in the *general fund,* which is also the object of most attention during budget preparation and adoption. GAAP also requires *special revenue funds* for revenues and spending from certain dedicated revenue sources, including federal funds and some earmarked taxes and fees. Spending on capital projects and major equipment purchases is reported in the *capital projects fund,* together with the dollars that have been received to fund that spending from bond proceeds or general revenues. Similarly, spending on interest and principal for state debt is accounted for in the *debt service fund,* together with revenues transferred from operating funds or dedicated taxes or fees. Finally, nongovernmental fund types are also used to account for pension funds and other funds held by the state for the benefit of employees or other government units.

Many state and local governments also require that financial reports be structured according to state or local laws. In those cases financial results according to this *statutory accounting* scheme would be included in a government's financial reports, along with cash and GAAP results. Annual financial reports are issued in a prescribed format called the *basic financial statements*

(BFS), which are accompanied by *required supplementary information* (RSI), including a discussion by management on operating results. These tables and their footnotes are part of a broader report called the *comprehensive annual financial report* (CAFR), which includes demographic and statistical data about the government in question.

After the fiscal year has closed these financial reports are prepared and issued by the state's *independent auditor,* who might be one of the Big Four accounting firms, a prominent firm within the state, or an independently elected comptroller or auditor. To receive an *unqualified* or *"clean" opinion* from the auditor, these reports must conform to GAAP. No equivalent sanction exists for governments whose budgets, as opposed to financial reports, are not presented in full conformance with GAAP, but the credit-rating agencies do prefer to see some GAAP overview of the budget, and many states present a GAAP financial plan in addition to cash-basis plans in their proposed budgets. Most budgets are presented using the governmental funds structure prescribed by GAAP. As a general rule states do not try to balance their budgets on a GAAP basis.

Budget Execution

Once a budget has been adopted by the legislature and the new fiscal year begins, state government begins to operate under that budget. Typically some items in the budget have been included as *lump sums,* and the budget office must make additional *allocations* of those funds before they can be spent. Initially those funds will be divided into amounts to be spent for personnel (usually called *personal services* [PS]) and spent for other purposes (sometimes called *other than personal services* [OTPS] or *nonpersonal services* [NPS]).

To avoid overspending during the fiscal year the budget office will sometimes dole out budgeted funds to the operating agencies in pieces, establishing *disbursement ceilings* or issuing *quarterly allocations* of agency funds. Those controls become stricter when the economy slumps or particularly risky budgets are enacted. The budget office also compares planned spending and receipts to actual outlays and collections. Where significant differences exist, the budget office will produce *variance reports* analyzing the reasons for those discrepancies and suggesting remedial action. The tighter the controls imposed during budget execution, the more frequent the complaints from agency heads about budget office *micromanagement.*

Debt

As discussed in memo 4, most governments choose to pay for all of their needs out of taxes and user charges. Others use debt to finance some or all of their capital projects. Under fiscal stress, governments sometimes use borrowing to finance imbalances between receipts and disbursements.

In general capital spending can be financed by operating funds transferred from the general fund, federal aid, dedicated taxes or fees, or bond proceeds. States may issue *general obligation* (GO) *bonds* for capital purposes, pledging the state's full faith and credit. Alternatively, they may issue less secure debt instruments, such as *appropriation-backed bonds* or *certificates of participation* (COPs) in state leases or contracts. GO bonds receive higher *credit ratings* than other types of debt from Moody's Investor Service, Standard & Poor's, and Fitch, the three companies that issue the most widely accepted ratings. Credit ratings are used by investors to simplify comparisons among governments, and they are based on several criteria, including debt load, economic strength, financial operations, and management capacity.

Governments issue long-term debt to finance capital projects and use short-term debt to finance *cash flow needs* created when the timing of receipts and the timing of disbursements are mismatched. When borrowing for cash flow purposes, a state might issue *tax anticipation notes* (TANs) or *revenue anticipation notes* (RANs).

In difficult fiscal circumstances a government might also borrow to meet the cash flow needs produced by deficits. Short-term securities issued for this purpose are usually called *deficit notes* or *budget notes*. A number of state governments, including New York, California, Massachusetts, and Connecticut, have also issued long-term bonds to fund out deficits accumulated over a period of several years.

Notes

1. The discussion below draws heavily for structure and inspiration on the "Financial Terminology" section of the *Citizen's Guide* produced by the New York State Division of the Budget. This material is available at www .budget.ny.gov/citizen/financial/glossary_all.html.

2. Summaries of statements detailing GAAP, together with explanatory material and examples of applications, are available on the website of the Governmental Accounting Standards Board (GASB) at www.gasb.org. See also Warren Ruppel, *Wiley GAAP for Governments 2011* (Hoboken, NJ: John Wiley & Sons, 2011), one of several reference guides to GAAP for state and local governments that are updated frequently.

Index